MY FRIEND THE ENEMY

My Friend the Enemy

An English Boy in Nazi Germany

PAUL BRISCOE

with Michael McMahon

First published in Great Britain
2007 by Aurum Press Ltd
7 Greenland Street, London NW1 0ND
www.aurumpress.co.uk

A catalogue record for this book is available from the British Library.

ISBN-10: 1 84513 231 9
ISBN-13: 978 1 84513 231 6

3 5 7 9 10 8 6 4
2007 2009 2011 2010 2008

Designed by Richard Marston
Typeset in Minion by SX Composing DTP, Rayleigh, Essex
Printed and bound in Great Britain by MPG Books, Bodmin, Cornwall

For my German family, especially Hildegard; and for my English family: Monica, Catherine and Robert – and my mother

CONTENTS

ACKNOWLEDGEMENTS

I would like to thank Geoff and Hilary Dellar, who encouraged me to make my first attempt at writing my story many years ago, and Ken Chaundler and Peter Chafer, who offered me such valuable friendship and support. I am doubly grateful to Molly Burkett of Barny Books, who published the first version of my memoirs, *Foster Fatherland*, and who introduced me to my agent, Jonathan Conway of Mulcahy and Viney Ltd, who has done much to bring this present project to completion. It was Jonathan who introduced me to my co-author Michael McMahon, who has helped me find the words that capture my memories so precisely, and to Karen Ings at Aurum, who has edited our joint efforts with such skill.

My wife, Monica, and our children, Catherine and Robert, have helped me in all sorts of ways, including contributing insights into their highly unusual mother-in-law and grand-mother. My first cousin, Angela Grayson, provided me with valuable information about Mother's family background, and a second cousin, Paul Dodwell, retrieved copies of Mother's police and MI5 files from the Public Record Office.

Among the books that I have found useful in researching Mother's activities in the 1930s and 1940s are Richard Griffiths' *Patriotism Perverted: Captain Ramsay, The Right Club and British Anti-Semitism 1939–40* (Constable, 1998), Richard Thurlow's *Fascism in Britain: A History 1918–1985* (Basil Blackwell, 1987) and the fascinating biography of Sir Oswald Mosley, *Blackshirt* (Viking Penguin, 2006) by Stephen Dorril, which has greatly helped me understand the politics of the period. I have also learned much from two excellent biographies of William Joyce: *Haw-Haw* by Nigel Farndale (Pan, 2005) and *Germany Calling* by Mary Kenny (New Island, 2004).

Paul Briscoe
February 2007

PREFACE

This story is true. All the events described actually happened, and all the dialogue that I quote is either as I remember hearing it, or as recorded by Special Branch and MI5 agents, in documents that are now available in the Public Record Office. I have used two other sources to recreate the story of my mother's life between the late 1930s and the end of the war: her unpublished autobiography, *Daemons and Magnets*, and her published novel *No Complaints in Hell* (Peter Davies, 1949), which contains the thinly disguised story of a part of her life that she was ashamed of, and never spoke about.

Kristallnacht

9–10 November 1938

At first, I thought I was dreaming, but then the rhythmic, rumbling roar that had been growing inside my head became too loud to be contained by sleep. I sat up to break its hold, but the noise got louder still. There was something monstrous outside my bedroom window. I was only eight years old, and I was afraid.

It was the sound of voices – shouting, ranting, chanting. I couldn't make out the words, but the hatred in the tone was unmistakable. There was also – and this puzzled me – excitement. For all my fear, I was drawn across the room to the window. I made a crack in the curtains and peered out. Below me, the triangular medieval marketplace had been flooded by a sea of heads, and flames were bobbing and floating between the caps and hats. The mob had come to Miltenberg, carrying firebrands, cudgels and sticks.

The rage of the crowd was directed at the small haberdasher's shop on the opposite side of the marketplace. Nobody was looking my way, so I dared to open the window a little, just enough to hear what all the shouting was about.

The words rushed in on the cold, late autumn air. '*Ju-den raus! Ju-den raus!*' – 'Jews out! Jews out!'

I didn't understand it. The shop was owned by Mira. Everybody in Miltenberg knew her. Mira wasn't a Jew, she was a person. She was Jewish, yes, but not like *the Jews*. They were dirty, subhuman, money-grubbing parasites – every schoolboy knew that – but Mira was – well, Mira: a little old woman who was polite and friendly if you spoke to her, but generally kept herself to herself. But the crowd didn't seem to know this: they must be outsiders. Nobody in Miltenberg could possibly have made such a mistake. I was frightened for her. The mob was yelling for her to come out, calling her 'Jew-girl' and 'pig' – '*Raus, du Jüdin, raus, du Schwein!*' – but I was willing her to stay put, to hide, to wait for them to go away: *No, Mira, don't come out, don't listen to them, please* . . .

A crash rang out. Someone had put a brick through her shop window. The top half of the pane hung for a moment, like a jagged guillotine, then fell to the pavement below. The crowd roared its approval, but the roar subsided as people began to nudge and point. Three storeys above them, a window was opened, and a pale, frightened face looked out. The window was level with mine, and I could see Mira very clearly. Her eyes were dark, like glistening currants.

The mob fell silent to let her speak, and her thin voice trembled over their heads. '*Was ist los? Warum all das?*' – 'What's going on? What's all this about?' But it was clear that she knew. A man in the crowd mimicked her in mocking falsetto, and the Marktplatz echoed with cruel laughter. Another voice yelled, '*Raus, raus, raus!*' and the cry was picked up and quickly became a chant. The call was irresistible. Soon, Mira was standing in the wrecked doorway of her shop, among the ribbons, reels and rolls of cloth that lay scattered among the broken glass. She was wearing a long white nightdress. The wind caught it, and it ballooned about her. Then she was gone, lost in the crowd, which moved off along the Hauptstrasse towards the middle of the town. Behind them, the marketplace filled with dark.

*

The next morning, our first lesson was interrupted by the appearance of Herr Göpfert, who strutted into our classroom with even more swagger than usual. He was wearing his Brownshirt uniform, which meant that he was on Party business. Short, fat, piggy-eyed Herr Göpfert had been our form teacher the previous year, so we all knew him for what he was – a bully. He had singled me out as one of his favourite victims. I had learned to bear the cut of the cane that he kept clipped under his desk, but I hadn't coped so well with the lash of his tongue. I had hung on his words so I wouldn't mis-understand his instructions, thus giving him an excuse to humiliate me for failing to carry them out. I had found the pain of being singled out for humiliation unbearable. I had been desperate to fit in, to be accepted, to be like the others – indeed, to be more like the others than they were. And Herr Göpfert knew this, which meant that he had been able to crush me as easily as he could screw up a piece of paper.

Upon his entrance we stood to attention and offered him the Party salute; he returned it and, as he lowered his arm, waved at us to sit. It was the same fussy little gesture that he had made at the beginning of every schoolday the previous year. The impatiently wagging hand accused us of not sitting down when we knew we were supposed to, but nobody dared to move before it wagged. We all recognised the simpering, self-satisfied lilt in his voice, but that morning he seemed smugger than ever. 'So,' he said, '*es kommt*' – 'So, the time has come.' Evidently, some historic moment had arrived, but nobody dared to ask what it was; making us wait to find out clearly gave him pleasure. The day's lessons had been cancelled, he informed us; we were to line up in front of the Volksschule*, where we would be told what to do.

Whatever was going to happen must have been planned well in advance, for the streets were lined with Brownshirts and Party officials, and the boys from the senior school were assembled in the uniform of the Hitler Youth. A festival atmosphere filled the town. Party flags, red, black and white, hung from first-floor windows, fluttering and snapping in the breeze – just as they did during the Führer's birthday celebrations each April. But there was something angry and threatening in the air, too.

A command was barked out and the older boys marched off, their boots clattering on the cobblestones. Our teachers ushered us youngsters in their wake. Kind, soft-featured Herr Arnold, who had taught me in my first year at school, looked solemn and uncomfortable as he fussed around the six-year-olds at the back. He was like a mother hen trying to round up

*Primary school

4

her chicks. Herr Göpfert, meanwhile, was swaggering and grinning, strolling along beside us, hands on hips, chest pushed out. He looked like a uniformed toad. We were still struggling to get our short legs to fall in with the pace of the seniors when the whole column was suddenly called to a halt.

Over the heads of the bigger boys in front of us, I could just see the portico of Miltenberg's tiny synagogue. I passed it every day on my way to and from school. It was a dark, tired-looking building, which seemed to want to shrink away from the street. Today, though, it was the focus of the whole town's attention. We all stood there staring at it while we waited to find out what was to happen next. For a long moment, nobody moved and all was quiet. Then, another command was shouted – I was too far back to make out the words – and the boys at the front broke ranks, flying at the synagogue entrance, cheering as they ran. When they reached the door, they clambered over each other to beat on it with their fists. I don't know whether they broke the lock or found a key, but suddenly another cheer went up as the door opened and the big boys rushed in. We youngsters stood still and silent, not knowing what to expect. Crashing and splintering sounds began to spill out onto the street from inside the building, accompanied by wild whoops and jeers. Suddenly, Herr Göpfert was standing in front of us. 'Go on,' he said. He had a twisted smile on his face. 'Go on. You go in, too!' We hung back, unsure of ourselves, but he drove us on with a look.

Inside was a scene of hysteria. Some of the seniors were on the balcony, tearing up books and throwing the pages in the air, where they drifted to the ground like leaves sinking through water. A group of them had got hold of a banister rail and kept rocking it back and forth until it broke. When it came away, they flung the spindles at the chandelier that hung over the centre of the room. Clusters of crystal fell to the floor. I stood there, transfixed by shock and disbelief. What they were doing was wrong: why weren't the adults telling them to stop?

And then it happened. A book thrown from the balcony landed at my feet. Without thinking, I picked it up and hurled it back. I was no longer an outsider looking on. I joined in, abandoning myself completely to my excitement. We all did. When we had broken all the chairs and benches into pieces, we picked up the pieces and smashed them, too. We cheered as a tall boy kicked the bottom panel of a door to splinters; a moment later, he appeared wearing a shawl and carrying a scroll. He clambered up to the edge of the unbanistered balcony, and began to make howling noises in mockery of Jewish prayers. We added our howls to his.

As our laughter subsided, we noticed that someone had come in through a side door and was watching us. It was the rabbi: a real, live Jew, just like the ones in our school textbooks. He was an old, small, weak-looking man with a long dark coat and black hat. His beard was black, too, but his face was white with terror. Every eye in the room turned to him. He opened his mouth to speak, but before the words came, the first thrown book had knocked his hat off. We drove him out through the main door where he had to run the gauntlet of the adults outside. Through the frame of the doorway I saw fists and sticks flailing down. It was like watching a film at the cinema, but being in the film at the same time. I caught close-ups of several of the faces that made up the mob. They were the faces of men that I saw every Sunday, courteously lifting their hats to each other as they filed into church.

1

Displaced Persons

1899–1933

Looking back on my life, I see that I have managed to find a lot of time in which to do as I like . . .
Norah Briscoe, *Daemons and Magnets*

Sitting in my Suffolk farmhouse kitchen nearly seven decades later, I find myself wondering whether the eight-year-old English boy who played a part in those terrible events can really have been me. Winter wheat is ripening in the fields outside the window, and the morning sun is warming my back. The postman has just called, leaving an electricity bill and some junk mail advertising double glazing. Monica is listening to *Desert Island Discs* in the spare room, where she is making up the bed for our daughter, Catherine, who is driving over from Wales to stay with us for the weekend. Nazi Germany seems not only a different time and place, but a different world. But that world was once mine, and the proof of that lies on the table in front of me in a large cardboard box.

I hesitate before opening it, because revisiting my tainted childhood is painful. In some ways, the best memories are the worst: I cannot enjoy them without guilt. Feeling the time-softened cover of my Hitler Youth *Leistungsbuch** reminds me of the day that I was issued with it. Even now, I think of it as one of the happiest days of my life. I could hardly wait for my tenth birthday to come so that I could become a junior HJ (Hitler-Jugend) member, or *Pimpf*. In the event, I didn't have to: there, in fading ink under the neat, rectangular stamp of the Miltenberg NSDAP,† the date is recorded as '20.4.1940' – Hitler's birthday, which came three months before mine. Tucked inside the book is the 1,000-metre running certificate awarded to me four years later. Above my name are the Führer's words, our motto: *Flink wie Windhunde, Zäh wie Leder, Hart wie Kruppstahl* – Swift as greyhounds, tough as leather, hard as Krupps steel. I wasn't swift, tough or hard, to be honest – but I was the proudest *Pimpf* in Miltenberg, because I felt I *belonged*.

That pride is obvious in my *Leistungsbuch* photograph; almost all the pictures in the box show me with a smile. Here's one of several snaps of me wearing lederhosen, a grinning five-year-old with my hands in my pockets. This other one was taken a year later: my grin has broadened and my hands are confidently on my hips. Everyone is beaming in these photographs of me with Hildegard and Seppl, Oma and Opa,‡

*Achievement book.
†*Nationalsozialistische Deutsche Arbeiterpartei* (National Socialist German Workers' Party).
‡I always called Seppl's parents 'Oma' (granny) and 'Opa' (grandpa).

and Maria and Willi, the extended German family that accepted me as one of their own. Look: here's another leder-hosen picture. You can see Oma's affection for me in the hand she is resting on my shoulder. And here I am dressed up as a cowboy for the *Fastnacht** carnival in 1938: all our heads are huddled together for the camera – that's Tante Lina, who ran the Brauerei Keller, and Siegfried, the local Nazi Party bigwig.

No, it wasn't the thought of seeing those old snapshots that made me reluctant to open the box. It was the bundle of papers underneath them all. I put it there after I first read it almost twenty years ago. Reading it then was like ripping a scab from an old wound. It is the typescript of Mother's unpublished autobiography. In order to write my own, I have to open that old wound again, for the story of my own damaged childhood begins with the story of the damaged childhood of my mother.

*

There are two versions of Mother's life story in that bundle. Under a neatly typed final version is a first draft on yellowing paper tied together with an old leather shoelace. Turning the pages now, I notice that some are typed on the back of copies of the duplicated letter that in later life Mother sent to people who had advertised unwanted pets: '*Your advertisement in the local paper shows that you have given thought, and spent money, to try to be sure that the animal you can no longer keep goes to a good home. I do ask you to give a little further care so that when*

*The German equivalent of Mardi Gras.

it leaves you it does not fall into wrong hands.' My own autobiography might have been rather different if she had shown
such care for me. These, and all the other pages, are ragged at
the right-hand edge, showing signs of having been turned and
re-turned frequently. There are countless crossings-out and
changes made in different pens and pencils. Mother was
clearly anxious to tell her story *precisely*. But what she wrote is
not precisely the truth. It is certainly not the whole truth.

Norah Constance Levinia Davies was born on 14 July 1899,
though neither name nor date of birth is reported in her book.
She calls herself Catherine Dee, the pen name she used for
much of her writing and journalism. She called the book
Daemons and Magnets, explaining inside that the title refers to
the external forces that drove or pulled her throughout her
life. The reader soon recognises this as part of a pattern of self-
deception, for it is obvious that the greatest daemon in
Mother's life was her selfishness. But the title is nevertheless
appropriate. It defines everybody in Mother's world by how
they affect her; she is not really interested in anyone else
beyond that.

Mother reveals much more about herself in *Daemons and
Magnets* than she can have realised, and even more by what
she leaves out than what she puts in. There is surely something
odd about an autobiographer who makes only passing
reference to her parents or childhood. What little Mother
records of hers is mentioned in the first 25 lines of the book:

At five years old I decided that I would be a violinist after
hearing Kubelik play at our Town Hall; and was given a violin

accordingly, and a teacher who did her furious best to make me one. True, the local paper singled me out the following year as 'a little mite of six years who, it will readily be granted without resorting to flattery, gave the treat of the evening in the shape of a selection from *Maritana* on the violin, for which she was most vociferously applauded and encored'. They were not sparing of either space or praise in those indulgent days, and a spate of performances followed which only ceased with gawky girlhood and the end of cherubic charm. With it went the dream of fame with the fiddle.

By that time, however, another decision loomed. For some time now I had been much impressed by the stout, stately figure seen at the children's parties and Mayoral functions at the Town Hall, pencil and pad in hand: our Lady Reporter. Her prestige was enormous; she was admitted everywhere free, with her fill of refreshments included. It seemed an ideal life to me and she appeared to thrive on it. I had no further doubts about the choice of a career.

How to attain it? The first surprise came when I divulged my plan at school-leaving age. One would think that such firmness of purpose would have been a cause of relief: not so. Family and nuns were aghast at the thought and the hazards implied.

The parents whom Mother hardly mentions were Catherine Dodwell, an Irish Catholic nurse who had given up her profession in 1897 to get married, and Adolf Davies, an accountant who worked for Lever Brothers.* Adolf – who was

---

*Lever Brothers manufactured Sunlight, the world's first packaged and branded laundry soap.

known at home as 'Addie' – allowed his children to be brought up as Catholics, though he remained a Protestant himself. The Davies family home was 213 Seaview Road, Wallasey, near Liverpool. It was a respectable Victorian villa: three storeys with bay windows, and an attic that would later house the maid that Addie would employ when his earnings increased. On the other side of the road was the municipal cemetery. The tram depot was just along the way, and trams clattered and clanged past the house.

My grandmother's life was centred on home and church; her husband's on work. This involved more than just the time spent at the office, for employment with Lever Brothers was a way of life. The company provided all sorts of social benefits and facilities, including an amateur theatre group, and Addie used to direct plays for it. His colleagues, who called him 'AJ', thought of him as a 'life and soul of the party' type, but at home, he showed a very different side of his character. He was stern, dogmatic and – I am sorry to say – mean.

Norah was my grandparents' first child. Their second, Hilda, was born a year later. Then, when Mother was three, triplets arrived, and everything suddenly changed. Grandmother couldn't cope. Grandfather could have afforded to employ domestic help, but he chose not to. Instead, he asked his two unmarried sisters, Til and Lil, to look after his eldest child until things got easier. Auntie Til and Auntie Lil* kept a 'boarding-house for gentlemen' at 7 Hamilton Square, Birkenhead. Their guests were professional bachelors who

---

*Their full names were Matilda and Elisabeth.

worked in the Camel Laird shipyards. Most of them were naval engineers and ships' architects. They were thoroughly respectable, and some were quite distinguished. One of them was a man they always called 'Mr John', who had helped design the *Ark Royal* and the *Mauritania*.*

Norah was the real-life doll that Til and Lil had always wanted. Mother's parents might have rejected her, but her aunts spoiled her thoroughly. A photograph taken of Mother when she was about four shows her standing in a photographer's studio, holding out the skirts of a pretty white lace dress. I can just imagine Til and Lil behind the camera, saying, 'That's right, dear, show everybody how pretty you are!' Til and Lil sent Mother to ballet lessons and took her to concerts, and they bought her the violin that she describes herself playing in the first paragraph of *Daemons and Magnets*.

When Mother was nine, she moved back in with her parents. She didn't tell them then of her ambition to become a Lady Reporter. She didn't tell anyone, in fact, until the end of her education at the Lingdale House Convent, Birkenhead. The nuns made it clear that they considered journalism an unsuitable profession for a young Catholic lady, and they tried to steer her towards teaching, but she wasn't having it. She sidestepped a confrontation by signing up for a course at a secretarial college. Her parents assumed that she intended to use the skills that she learned there to get a job as a secretary. But Mother had other plans, which she kept to herself.

*When he retired, he bought a house in North Wales, and Til and Lil moved in to look after him. He left them the house in his will.

Job opportunities for women in journalism were rare in the 1920s; when Mother finished the course, which she hated, she took a job in an insurance office – which she hated even more. She writes of how she loathed the drudgery of it and how much she despised her new colleagues for 'leaping from their stools whenever a bell pinged, with the "Sir" ever ready to spring to their lips'. She couldn't stand the pettiness of office life. At the same time she was terrified of the managing director, who had a pointed white beard, and whose blood, Mother imagined, was 'white and icicle-sharp', too. His equally sharp-tongued secretary used to rummage through Mother's wastepaper basket at the end of each day and tell her off for spoiling too many letters. Mother felt bullied and degraded. The only colour to brighten the wretched routine was provided by the curses of the man who dictated letters at a nearby desk, whose favourite oath was '*God's trousers!*'

Mother couldn't stand this job for long, and after an equally unhappy spell as a secretary to two Scottish businessmen, she joined what she calls 'the female hive of a vast firm's export department'. It was a typing pool. She almost drowned in it. She found the work worthless, frustrating and very much beneath her dignity. She writes, 'It gave me an insight into the wasteful routine of memo and letter writing on the flimsiest of pretexts, which kept dozens of girls hammering at their machines all day, at the behest of semi-literate section managers concocting fresh outbursts of verbiage. I cannot think what else it gave me, beyond the prescribed twenty-one shillings a week, except plenty of typing practice.'

That practice was soon to be of use. Mother decided it was

time to fulfil her childhood resolution, so she wrote to the only journalist she knew, who was an old family friend she hadn't seen since childhood. He was a night editor on the *Liverpool Echo*, and he invited her to call at his office. The moment that Mother entered the building, she felt she was in her element.

> The throb of the machines and smell of printers' ink, the sounds and sights of nocturnal activity when ordinary folk were getting into their carpet slippers; the nonchalant manner of the commissionaire who directed me upstairs; the disorder discovered there when I opened the door of a paper-cluttered room, took me, as I thought, to the heart of Bohemia, to which I by rights belonged.

Mother's 'old family friend' – she doesn't name him – tried to discourage her, but she wouldn't be put off. She persuaded the editor of the *Echo* to give her a trial apprenticeship, during which she was more or less left to train herself. The pay was a pittance, but her mother helped her out by supplementing it – and agreeing to keep the new job secret from Addie until a suitable moment arrived. Unfortunately, he found out first, by chance:

> The storm was pretty tempestuous, but soon over; and in the end he came to be quite proud, I heard, of my modest achievements in print.

'*I heard.*' No normal person would report an estrangement from a parent in a passing remark like that. The only time Mother refers to her father again is to mention that by a certain time later in her life, he 'had died'. She doesn't say how it happened, or how she or anyone else was affected by his death.* I am not sure which other readers would find more shocking – her obvious lack of feeling for him, or the fact that she doesn't see the need to account for it. Readers of *Daemons and Magnets*, of course, wouldn't know that Mother had been farmed out as a child, which would explain why she was unable to feel normal human sympathy for a father who she felt had rejected her.

But the damage ran deeper than that. As a young woman, Mother seems to have shown little sign of normal human sympathy for anybody. Just before she left the *Liverpool Echo* to move to London, she was sent to report on a pitiful murder. An eleven-year-old girl had been raped, strangled and dumped down by the docks. When news got out, the police prevented the press from approaching the child's distressed parents, but when the Lady Mayor arrived to offer her condolences, she noticed Mother in the crowd of male reporters that had gathered outside. Thinking that another woman would help her comfort the grieving relatives, she invited Mother to join her. I don't know what support Mother provided, but her account does not suggest it was much:

Pregnant mother, with a soft Scottish burr to her voice as she poured out her tragic tale, angry husband denouncing fiendish

*Addie died in 1947. The obituary in the January 1948 edition of the Unilever house magazine, *Port Sunlight News*, records: 'He loved to talk of boyhood days, playing cricket in Hamilton Square Gardens with the FE Smith who was to become Lord Birkenhead and a hero of AJ's'.

neighbours and pestering newsmen, little brothers and sisters shyly peeping around their mother's skirt, Mayor's womanly words of sympathy . . . I got a story that was the envy of all the shivering sleuths outside.

Mother's interest was not in the fate of the child or the grief of the family, but in the fact that she managed to get a brilliant scoop.

In 1925, Mother moved south and joined the staff of the *Croydon Advertiser*. During the working week, she wrote what she was told to write, but in her free time, she wrote a number of comment pieces and short stories that reflected her thoughts on life. Mother always kept cuttings of her bylined work, though there were not many to keep during this period. The frustration she must have felt is expressed in one story that was accepted, a story that appeared in the November/December 1928 issue of a magazine called *The Quill*. The heroine is a woman born with the 'lamentable kink' of a talent for writing that society does not recognise: 'How she hated the thud of fat envelopes on the door mat! How she sickened at the sight of her own type-script at least twice a week!'

Two of Mother's pieces that were not rejected discussed marriage, a subject that had begun to loom large in her imagination as she approached the age of 30. A short story called 'The Glimpse', published in *Feminine Life*, is about a sparky woman trapped in domestic drudgery. Mother clearly didn't want that to happen to her. An opinion piece she wrote for the *Birmingham Mail* in 1928, under the title 'Working Partners', set out what she did expect of a husband and marriage:

The ideal husband for a wage-earning wife exists. He has evolved out of the war and post-war life – a tolerant, kindly, adaptable being with a philosophy of his own.

Mother must have recognised these qualities in Reginald Robert Briscoe, for she married him in 1929. But the marriage was doomed from the start. I have no memory whatsoever of my father, but Mother told me later that he had simple, domestic interests – his garden, his wire-haired terriers and his car. Mother wanted adventure, but the most adventurous thing her new husband ever did was to improvise on the piano at the local pub. All her life, she was driven by the belief that she was a cut above the ordinary; she had made the mistake of marrying a man who was ordinariness itself.

My father was a clerk in the Ministry of Works, though Mother mentions neither his name nor his profession in *Daemons and Magnets*. The book is full of extended descriptions of chance meetings with strangers, but she doesn't mention how or when she met her husband, and says nothing of courtship or falling in love. She devotes more words to describing her employers' opposition to the idea that their 'Lady Reporter' should get married than to the three years of the marriage itself. This is all she says about it, and the man she married:

The time came when, forsaking the busy newspaper world, I retired into the domestic one, no less busy but considerably less varied, to have a baby myself.* And so it came about that one bright spring morning, having put him out in his pram and looked round at the bright new houses, replicas of our own, identical except for the varying tastes in front gardens and paint-work, I realised that . . . home with me would never come first or be all-sufficing. I remember sitting down at the foot of the stairs, when I went in, overwhelmed by this moment of lucidity. Somebody, something, must surely get me out of this trap I had got myself into. I had never applied to my daemons in vain.

Spring faded into summer and nothing happened. I had some success with story writing, but nothing spectacular; and at last August came, a month I have never liked much. Its explosive force which lies hidden behind a deceptive calm has always worried me, and made September a welcome visitor. That summer† was a particularly hot one, and on a stifling August evening after a hard day's work in the garden – he was on leave from the office – my husband complained of feeling ill. We thought it might be a touch of sun-stroke, or the effects of the green apples eaten earlier, but the pains grew worse, and late that night, the doctor was called and hurried him off to hospital for an emergency operation for appendicitis. A violent thunderstorm raged after he had gone, and his favourite dog, disturbed at seeing him go off in the ambulance, kept up a wolfish howl throughout the night. I can hear the spine-chilling sound now, and see the lightning flashes slithering across the bedroom floor like evil smiles.

---

*I was born in July 1930. I think it says something about Mother that in my own autobiography, I find myself recording my own birth in a footnote! †1932.

He died a week later, on a day when the garden he loved was ablaze with marigolds. Not long before he died he told me that no matter how hard he tried to visualise the future, he could see none for himself although he had recently had promotion, and he was by no means a pessimistic character.

Widows who throw themselves on their husbands' funeral pyres are, at any rate, spared the pangs of remorse. I who had railed against my prison bars was racked by it now, and at last, unable to bear it, sent out a desperate plea for help. It was on the day after the funeral and I spoke to my husband as if he were alive in the room. Closing my eyes, I recounted the problems, then, one by one: the mortgage, the need to find work, someone to look after the child; but first, to be rid of that millstone, the house, which I couldn't afford to live in, and didn't want any more.

He was always ingenious in a crisis, had an instinct about people to go to in an emergency, could always find a roof in an unknown town. And as I continued my silent pleading I had a distinct conviction that I was being listened to. He had nothing to do with the grave now, death and its awful trappings were over and done with. He was wanting to help, to ease the burden of so sudden and unexpected a going. I felt very peaceful suddenly and freed of the burden of worry.

I think Mother left out of her autobiography the things that she was ashamed of and the things that did not make her seem special. I don't think she was trying to deceive the reader; I think she was trying to deceive herself – and in that she succeeded. She describes how she won applause as a child

21

violinist; she does not say who bought her the violin, paid for the lessons, and gave her the love and encouragement that inspired her confidence. It doesn't seem to matter; what matters is that it was Mother who got the applause.

I also think that she didn't realise how cold some of what she wrote would make her seem to others. She seems to have had a kind of emotional blind spot. Shortly after my father died, she wrote a piece about widowhood that was published in the *Evening Standard* of 27 April 1933. The piece was given the title 'Here is a Problem'. She wrote it under her maiden name, which seems to distance her even further from my father. In it, she laments the loss not of a loved one, but of a breadwinner. She rails against the 'irresponsibility' of a husband who does not take out life insurance, leaving his widow 'suddenly destitute'. She criticises parents who do not equip a daughter with 'every possible educational advantage in preparation for life's emergencies', which 'would stand her in good stead should her marriage end in disaster with the problem before her of how to be father and mother and breadwinner combined'. She phrases her complaints generally, but makes it clear that she is writing from personal experience.

Mother's solution to the problem that she describes so bitterly was to employ a nanny to look after me, and to get herself a job. Addie used his influence to get her into the PR department of Unilever, into which Lever Brothers had mutated after a merger. Mother says nothing of this assistance in *Daemons and Magnets*. Nor does she say anything about my nanny, who was clearly not an important person in Mother's life, though she certainly was in mine. Beatrice was large, round and deaf – and I loved her. She spoiled me utterly. Whatever I asked her for, I got double. More importantly, she provided me with the affection that every child needs. I do not remember ever once being embraced or kissed by Mother, but I cannot picture Beatrice without thinking of her gentle, loving hugs. Every morning, she would come with me in the taxi that took me to the Rudolf Steiner kindergarten, where I played with clay and sand and water. Then, when the weather permitted, she would take me to play in the park. When I was with Beatrice, I felt confident, happy and safe.

Mother, meanwhile, was determined to re-establish herself as a freelance journalist. When she came home from work in the evenings, I hardly saw her, for she would shut herself away to write the fiction and features she offered to newspapers and magazines. Two were accepted by a women's journal called *Home Making*. There, among advertisements for Snowfire face powder, Danderine hair beautifier, Symington's jelly crystals and Pul-front corsets, Mother's short story 'Last Romance' appeared in June 1933. It is about a wife who resents being left at home to bring up the baby while her husband pursues a successful career. The following September, the same magazine published a piece by Mother called 'When I am a Mother-in Law', in which she talks about her hopes for me when I grow up. 'I am certainly not jealous of the love that my son may one day give to a woman other than myself,' she writes; '. . . to have first place in the heart of a "Mother's Darling" is not my idea of achievement.'

2

Love at First Sight

1934–36

*My Dear Führer, I have watched with understanding
and interest the progress of your great and superhuman
work in regenerating your country.*
Lord Rothermere, letter to Adolf Hitler*

Mother might not have mourned for her husband, but she did
go into mourning for herself. My father's death had left her in
an awkward predicament, and she found herself feeling
anxious and depressed. In early 1934, she went for help to her
doctor. He told her she was suffering from 'delayed-action
strain' and prescribed a break. She decided to take a holiday
on the Continent, leaving me behind with Beatrice. She
invited her sister Hilda to join her, and Hilda left her own son,
Robin, with Beatrice, too.

Mother had no particular destination in mind until she
bumped into a work colleague by chance on a train. When the

*June 1939.

colleague recommended a particular guest house in Bavaria, Mother took it as 'a definite direction, as clear as a signpost', and she followed it. At the time, there was a lot of interest in political events taking place in Germany, where Hitler had been in power since January 1933. English people were discouraged from going there. Mother saw this as a challenge. She didn't believe half of what was being said about the Nazis in the papers, which had reported the imprisonment of thousands of dissenters, the dissolution of rival political parties, the dismissal of Jews from the civil service, and an official boycott of Jewish businesses. It is clear from what Mother writes in *Daemons and Magnets* that when she got to Germany, she saw only what she wanted to see:

> We seemed to have found in that other land of mountains and streams and towering forests, a corner of the world as remote from war and evil as was possible. Monks drove their oxen and primitive ploughs in the valleys, brewed beer, walked the streets unmolested, and weren't incarcerated by an atheistic state as one had read; here, the Middle Ages blended with the twentieth century; they were not an encrusted thing of the past. You could pray, dance, drink, smoke, and worship as you pleased. Young men in leather breeches leaped over flames on Midsummer Night in a pagan ritual and heard Mass next day. You could follow any creed you liked – provided you followed the Führer, too. And whose business was that but their own?

The naivety of that judgement is astonishing, but then love is blind, and Mother was falling in love – not with a person, but with a country and a political creed. Then she had a

chance encounter that made the daemonic magnetism of
Nazism irresistible.

One day we returned from a walk to find the village bedecked
everywhere with the Flag. The swastika fluttered from our bedroom window, bold black and red and white, and our landlady
hurried out to meet us to tell us the glad news. Two important
visitors were expected that afternoon, and were to stay at her
inn. They had relatives in the neighbourhood and were passing
through the village on the way to Party Headquarters in order to
meet them. Yes, they were two distinguished Party members,
and in due course, all eyes were to follow us reverently as we
were summoned to drink with them. There was much heel-
clicking, and many bows and smiles over the liberal supplies of
wine, as neither of the distinguished guests could speak English,
and we no German. The manner of one of them became
distinctly less formal as the wine flowed, and my pretty sister's
spell began to work, unknown and unwanted by her. One of
them sat slumped in his chair, gazing at us through hooded eyes.
His breast was covered in medals, and he was clearly the more
important one, although obese and unhealthy looking. With an
imperious snap of the fingers he suddenly sprang into action
and led the company (now uniformed to a man) in the Horst
Wessel Song, and then, to our astonishment and embarrassed
smiles, in 'God Save the King'. After that, with another flick of
the fingers, a young man sitting unobtrusively behind him was
summoned to his side, and promptly lifted the squatting figure
in his arms and carried it, legs uselessly dangling, to the door,
while the company with upraised arms uttered the familiar cry;

and he was gone, a man turned ventriloquist's doll, to be carried upstairs to bed.* He had been shot in the back during the Munich Putsch, and was paralysed from the waist downwards, an honoured pillar of the Party, and permanently tended by his young valet-chauffeur-bodyguard.

The next day further honours were piled on us in the interests of Anglo-German friendship. We were invited to accompany the famous pair on their visit to the relatives. When I look back on it now, and know the German official character better, I realise what a signal honour this was, and how little we appreciated it, as through the village streets we drove, with every hand upraised, hallowed, foreigners though we were, by the mystique of the little enamel Flag on the bonnet of the car. Our smiles and bows gradually improved as self-consciousness gave way to self-importance. It is easy to see how the humble and insignificant can be exalted by the automatic glory of a Flag which doesn't even belong to them, and which they have been urged to hate. How much easier the exaltation for those to whom it belongs!

Mother had found a flag that offered her the recognition she felt was hers by right, the recognition denied to her by her family and by society. By the time she stepped out of that car with cheering ringing in her ears, she was ready to embrace a new political philosophy with a passion that she could never bring to human relationships. It was a good match, for

*I have been unable to identify this character as one of those injured in the failed coup of 8 November 1923. It may be that Mother is mistaken, and the man was injured in one of the many other violent events of those times.

Nazism did not count a lack of sympathy for other people's feelings as a weakness; rather, it was seen as a strength.

Mother's encounter with National Socialism in Germany was immediately followed by an introduction to its English equivalent. Shortly after she got back to her desk at Unilever, she was ordered to go through all the newspapers published by the Harmsworth Press in the previous six months and collect all the references to Sir Oswald Mosley, the English Fascist leader. She later learned that the cuttings had been requested by some Jewish directors of Unilever who had decided to present Harmsworth's owner, Lord Rothermere, with an ultimatum: if he did not stop backing Mosley, they and their friends would stop placing advertisements in his papers. In the event, Rothermere gave in. Meanwhile, Mother had found herself reading almost everything favourable that had been written recently about Mosley and his Blackshirts.* What she read, she liked.

But it was fascism in power that had captured Mother's heart and imagination. A 'longing for Germany' had seized her 'to the exclusion of all thoughts of security, caution and common sense'. She handed in her notice at Unilever and resolved to support herself – and me – on whatever income she could earn by freelance journalism, leaving her free to make several return trips to a land on which fascism was rapidly tightening its grip.

After one of these visits, she told Beatrice and me that we

---

*In January 1934 the *Daily Mail* carried a piece written by Rothermere under the headline 'Hurrah for the Blackshirts!'.

were to receive a German she had met as a guest. She introduced Seppl as someone who had come over to improve his English, but I saw him as an intruder and took an instant dislike to him. I resented this tall, dapper man with a studied smile and big eyes framed by round, black spectacles. I had been used to being the centre of attention and getting my own way. Suddenly, there was someone in my life who used the word 'no'.

When Mother announced that Seppl had invited us to come to Germany, and Seppl told me he would soon make a man of me, I knew that my instincts had been right. I didn't want to go to a country full of people like him; and I certainly didn't need him or anyone else to make a man of me. Where Mother went didn't matter, but I couldn't bear the thought of being separated from Beatrice. My feelings on the matter are obvious in the studio photograph that was taken of Mother and me in early 1935, just before we set off for Germany. Mother is staring at the camera and paying no attention to me at all. I am standing behind her with my hand resting nervously on her shoulder. She looks cold, confident and completely self-contained; I look just how I felt: lonely and afraid.*

We travelled to Germany by aeroplane. I can't remember setting off – I suppose we must have flown from Croydon – but I remember the flight itself vividly. The weather was fierce and the plane felt frighteningly flimsy. Straight after take-off, we were thrown about terribly, and when we broke our journey in Belgium, high winds made landing difficult. I

*The photograph appears on the back cover of this book.

looked out of the window and saw men running along beside us, throwing ropes over the wings and holding on to them to slow us down. I was certain that we were going to be blown over, but just before we got to the end of the runway, we lurched to a halt. When we took off again I needed to go to the toilet, but when I lifted the lid and saw the fields and houses rushing by beneath, I decided it could wait.

*

The rocking of the train is making me feel drowsy. If it weren't for Mother's elbow pressed into my shoulder, I would fall asleep. On the other side of me is a fat man whose side is so soft and shapeless that it half swallows me. I am too tightly pinned to be able to tilt forward to see his face, and I can feel his body expand and contract as he breathes. Every in-breath is a faint, whistling wheeze; every out-breath a fainter sigh. On the lap of the woman sitting opposite me is a wicker basket. Through its loosely woven sides, I watch a chicken jerking its head from side to side. Above it, the woman's head nods in and out of sleep. To the left of her, the lips of two old men are moving gently, but the sounds that come from their mouths make no sense. One of them produces a sausage from a paper bag and cuts into it with a penknife. The air in the carriage smells of spices, chicken droppings and sweat.

*

Miltenberg was at the end of the line. When the slow train finally got there, a blue-coated stationmaster with a gold-braided hat was marching along the platform blowing his whistle and shouting something that must have meant 'everybody out'. Mother and I gathered up our baggage and tumbled into a taxi that took us to the centre of town, where it dropped us outside the Brauerei Keller, the old inn where we were to stay. Standing in the doorway, framed by geraniums in flowerpots, was a tall woman with a big smile and dark, swept-back hair. She shook Mother's hand, and then picked me up, hugged me to her bosom and held me in her arms. I didn't understand the words she spoke to me, but I could tell that they were welcoming and kind. 'This is Tante Lina,' said Mother. '*Tante* is German for "aunt".' I warmed to Tante Lina immediately. She was like Beatrice.

We stayed at the Brauerei Keller for several weeks. After a while, Tante Lina arranged for me to play with some local children. I soon picked up a handful of words in the local dialect. Unfortunately, they were not words that I could use to advantage. My new playmates taught me to recite short, guttural incantations until I pronounced them perfectly; when I repeated them back at the inn, Tante Lina covered her face in embarrassment. Mother, meanwhile, was feeling more and more at home. She describes our time at the Brauerei Keller in *Daemons and Magnets*:

> It cost very little more than the rent for the flat in England for both of us to be housed and fed at our inn, and life was never without interest of some kind. There was a constant stream of visitors, travellers on business and for pleasure. Sometimes the odd English traveller would appear, curious, as I had been, to see how things were for themselves. They would ask me how I

was 'treated' and showed surprise when I denied all knowledge of the police, secret or otherwise. My valiant sister joined us for a long and happy stay while her child was away at school, and altogether it was an extremely happy summer.

In the autumn of 1935, Mother decided that she wanted to see more of Germany. We would start our tour by spending some time in Frankfurt. When we arrived at the station, she went to a hairdresser's to freshen up after the journey, and one of the assistants recommended the Pension Weber, where we took a large double room at the top of seven flights of stairs. It was good value: full board cost the equivalent of thirty shillings a week for her, and half that for me.

Mother arranged for me to go to a local kindergarten. It was not a happy experience. The little German I knew was no use to me, and I had no idea how to get myself accepted as a member of the group. Perhaps some of the children tried to be welcoming – I can't remember. But if they did, I had neither the language nor the confidence to respond, and I was soon being teased as a misfit. When the others made a ring round me to taunt me, I would raise my fists and square up to them. Then, they would chant '*Schmeling! Schmeling!*' at me until I had to fight back tears of frustration and rage. I thought they were telling me I was smelly; I didn't know they were comparing me to Max Schmeling, the champion boxer.* One day

---

*I have since discovered something that people didn't know at the time: Max Schmeling was passionately opposed to Nazism. He sheltered two Jewish youngsters in his hotel room during *Kristallnacht*, and later helped them flee the country.

I came home full of excitement, believing that at last, I had been accepted. I had been given a part in a play called *Ten Little Nigger Boys*: I was Nigger Boy number eleven, in case someone was ill. But on the day of the performance, all the cast turned up, and I was left watching from the wings with nothing to do and nobody to comfort me in my disappointment. Mother had been too busy to attend.

Life was not quite so difficult for me back at the Pension Weber, where, as the only child, I was petted and patronised by the other guests. Many of them were English couples and individuals on tours led by Molly Hiscox, a pretty woman in her late twenties who organised German holidays for English Fascist sympathisers. Mother and Molly found that they shared an interest in spiritualism, and they quickly became friends, for reasons that Mother makes clear in *Daemons and Magnets*:

> Neither of us liked the unfair anti-German talk that was increasing in intensity in England . . . True, Austen Chamberlain had just returned from a visit to announce that Germany was 'one vast arsenal'. What of it? Must they not take proper precautions to protect themselves? But weren't the majority of its inhabitants – and Molly travelled widely in Germany and saw them for herself – enjoying life as they hadn't enjoyed it for many years, with good roads to drive on in their cheap and well-made little cars, a freedom from industrial troubles, a decrease in violence, a return to sanity and security, in fact? They were borne on an upsurge of hope and confidence, freed from the long, lingering misery of defeat, we agreed.

. . . We had to admit that the women's clothes were a trifle behind the times, that people's mobility was strictly controlled, and that freedom as we had been trained to understand it was certainly lacking; but these things were part of the birth pangs, and would improve as the economy became stable, and full stature was regained . . .

. . . In the meantime, we listened to the tramp of marching soldiers in the streets at intervals, and found their triumphant songs and happy faces immensely heartening. Here was real joy through strength.* We heard no menace in them, nor in the mock air-raids and blacked-out rehearsals that occasionally occurred. The Germans were realists.

An encounter with the Gestapo, no less, gave me one more proof of the perfidy of the detractors. The two men who called for me were insignificant looking enough. Only Frau B's† flurried manner and anxious eyes as she ushered me into their presence warned me that they were not as they seemed; and the swift turning back of the jacket lapels‡ gave the final theatrical touch. Neither could speak English, nor could their chief, to whose bureau they accompanied me on foot. Whether I got anything across in my execrable German of my admiration for their country, I don't know. At all events, the handsome man with the grey, clipped moustache, appraising me from behind his desk, had soon had enough of me, abruptly shook my hand,

*The expression that Mother echoes here is 'Strength through Joy' (*Kraft durch Freude*), the name of the Nazi scheme that provided holidays and leisure activities for workers.
†Presumably this is Mother's landlady.
‡To show their badges?

and had me taken away, not to an extermination camp, but out into the street and freedom. I had been confused, so far as I could gather from their questioning, with an English person who had been writing uncomplimentary things about Germany to a Danish friend, and for a moment, a stab of worry had marred the interview, but true innocence has a disarming way with it, and lends a kind of arrogance, and I carried off that interview with aplomb, I thought. And that was the last I heard or saw of the handsome man and his underlings. The big bad German wolf was a myth. This Little Red Riding Hood had known it all along, and went on her way unscathed by doubt or fear.

I wish I could say that later in *Daemons and Magnets* Mother dismisses these extraordinary judgements as mistaken, but she doesn't. The tone of the book is odd, but it is not ironic. It is as if she is saying, 'This is how I saw it, and that's that,' not 'This is how I saw it – how wrong I was!' To that extent, *Daemons and Magnets* is honestly written: the author is just not interested in how her beliefs and actions affect other people, and it does not occur to her that a reader might find that strange.

At this time, of course, I was completely unaware of the adult world of politics, but I was beginning to understand something about the adult world of money. The ups and downs of Mother's income from freelance journalism were reflected in the rooms we took as we travelled about the country. When funds were low, the pensions became tattier and the rooms got smaller and higher up – on the second or third floor, and sometimes under the roof. The smallest room I can remember was an attic in Stuttgart, where I spent several weeks ill in bed, suffering from chickenpox. It was only when I read *Daemons and Magnets* that I learned that my illness had kept us in that 'dreary pension' for a period that included Christmas Day, 1935. Mother writes that we didn't even get a hot meal, because the cook had been given the day off. I don't suppose I missed it – I felt too ill. What I do remember is that shortly afterwards, we were visited by Seppl and a friend of his, who brought me some marzipan sweets in the shape of animals. Mother makes no mention of this in her book.

At the end of each month, Mother kept enough money back for a return trip to England, where she would take the articles she had written to her agent and seek out more commissions. She usually returned with some cash, but it would quickly run out, and she would then wait anxiously for further payments to arrive in the post. Even as a five-year-old, I could recognise her anxiety, and I once saw her rip open an envelope so desperately that she tore all the banknotes inside.

I looked forward to Mother's trips to England, because when she was away I was taken to stay with Seppl's family in Miltenberg. I loved it there. It was a fairy-tale illustration come to life. Its narrow, cobbled streets of ancient, timber-framed buildings stood huddled under a handsome castle perched among densely wooded hills. Boats and barges of all shapes and sizes drifted down a broad, dark river spanned by a fine stone bridge. There, for a few days at a time, I didn't have to live out of a suitcase in an anonymous guest house, but could relax in a real family home. With each visit, that home and the family that lived there felt more and more my own. The resentment I had felt toward Seppl faded and then turned to admiration. I was particularly impressed by his motorbike; he used to sit me on the seat so that I could pretend I was riding it.

Seppl, his sister Maria and their mother and stepfather, Oma and Opa Sauter, lived in a large apartment above the family's four-storey furniture shop on Miltenberg's Marktplatz. The business was called Möbelhaus* Weyrich, Weyrich being the name of Oma's first husband. It was housed in a remarkable building. It had once been as ornately timbered as the houses around it, but after a fire in the nineteenth century it had been rebuilt with a smoothly rendered front. From the outside, the place looked bland and symmetrical, but the interior was an irregular warren of interconnecting showrooms, offices, storerooms, parlours, pantries, passages, cellars, attics, workshops, cupboards and staircases built into the hillside behind. It was a wonderful place to explore, and I was given free run of it.

To me, it seemed more like a little town than an individual property: at the heart of it, in the middle of the first floor, was a glazed courtyard that was like a village square. Downstairs, the main entrance hall was wide enough to contain the family car, Seppl's motorbike, an old pram, a pushchair, several redundant armchairs, and dozens of rolls of the brown linoleum that was offered for sale in the shop. The entrance hall to the living accommodation was on the second storey at

*Furniture House.

the back. It was equally cluttered – as was the rest of the house, in which bales of curtain material, reels of upholstery webbing and boxes of fantastically shaped tools and fixtures lined the sides of all the passages and filled every corner and shelf.

The family's domestic and business lives overlapped completely, and the living room was as chaotic as everywhere else. A roll-top desk stuffed with business papers was flanked by yet more rolls of lino and an upright piano covered in piles of invoices, bills and trade catalogues. In the corner was a *Kachelofen*, a tall, tiled wood stove that stood almost as high as the ceiling. On winter evenings, the family would gather round it – and talk shop.

When Mother returned from England, I would be snatched from this fascinating environment and the two of us would be on the road again. Each time, I resented it more. It was no way to bring up a child, but Mother didn't see it like that. She thought herself the very model of modern parenthood, and wrote newspaper articles offering advice to other parents. One of these pieces, published in the *Daily Mirror* in 1935, appears under a chocolate-box photograph of me holding a dandelion. The headline asks what a mother should tell her child about religion. Mother answers by describing what she has told me. 'Organised religion,' she writes, 'is not for my son.' She has not passed on the 'half truths, muddled legends and negative teaching' that she learned in her own childhood, but taught her son 'a religion of [her] own making'.

He has been instilled with a profound respect for the earth which gives him his food and nourishes the flowers and trees.

The moon and the stars also arouse in him a lively interest and fascination. The elements are a source of wonder, but not of fear . . . For him there is no unknown Presence lurking in the shadows whose anger has been roused by the sins of the day . . . He has never heard the word 'Sin'.*

Mother writes that the religion she has made up for me does allow for the possibility, at least, of there being a creator God, and a historical Christ who tried 'to teach people how they should live and be happy'. But she has not, she writes, told her five-year-old son of the Crucifixion. She would 'prefer any information of this kind to be kept from him until he begins dimly to understand the meaning of mob cruelty'.

If the people who read this had known how Mother was actually bringing me up at the time, not many of them would have thought her qualified to offer advice on parenting. The picture she paints of a spiritual bond with me is utterly false. I hardly ever saw her, and when I did, I was made to feel that my very existence was an obstruction to her work. The year after that piece was published, she left me in the keeping of a family that would bring me up as a Roman Catholic – the very religion she claimed to have rejected – in a country where I would come to 'understand the meaning of mob cruelty' by taking an active part in it.

*The historian Stephen Dorril tells me that this type of philosophy was common to many of the Fascists of the time. He calls it 'a kind of egotistical New Ageism'.

3

Fitting In

1936–37

*There is a kind of magic associated with the names of
some ancient towns. There is an air of mystery about
them.* *

700 Jahre der Stadt Miltenberg am Main, 1937

Mother couldn't keep carrying me about like a suitcase for
ever. In the summer of 1936 I turned six, the age at which
German children had to go to school. When she left me with
Seppl, Oma, Opa and Maria in the spring, she explained that
this time, I would be staying with them for good. I was to start
at the Miltenberg Volksschule the following September. Meanwhile, she would carry on travelling and writing, but would
come back as often as she could. Later, she would join us
permanently, and then the family would be complete. It didn't
occur to me that this meant that Mother planned to marry

---

*'Der Name mancher alten Stadt ist von einem eigenen Zauber umwittert.
Geheimnis ist um sie.'

Seppl, but if I had been told, I wouldn't have objected, for I had grown to like him, and already looked upon him as a father.

Seppl was charming, and he knew it. He certainly charmed me. I soon forgot the resentment I had felt when he had first appeared in my life. He would joke with me and tease me good-naturedly, and even before I had much grasp of German I never had any difficulty understanding him. He was confident and relaxed, and made people feel at ease in his company. His clothes always seemed smarter than everyone else's, and his hair more perfectly groomed. I didn't know the meaning of the word 'style' then, but I could see that there was something about his appearance that made him stand out in a crowd, as if he alone were sharply in focus. I admired him, and he indulged me by allowing me to follow him about. When I accompanied him on various errands around and about Miltenberg, I was proud to be with this important man that everyone knew and liked.

The ladies in particular seemed to like Seppl. Even as a six-year-old I could see that. He would say things to women that would make them smile and blush. As my German got better, I began to understand why. '*Na, du schöne, wie geht's?*'* he would say to a pretty stranger. Sometimes, when a girl passed, he would turn to me and say, '*Guck dir den Hintern an von Der!*'† I obediently looked, but only to please him.

Seppl hardly had the makings of an ideal husband, but I can see how easy it must have been for Mother to fall for him. He

*'Now then, my pretty, how are you?'
†'Look at the backside on that one!'

was fun. He was the very opposite of my domesticated, desk-bound father. Seppl travelled the country, doing deals and taking risks. It later turned out that quite a number of those risks involved other women. I don't know when it was that Mother realised this, because in later life, she never spoke of her relationship with Seppl. She makes no mention of him in *Daemons and Magnets*, even though in January 1936 she wrote to the Foreign Office to announce her intention to marry him, and to ask how her nationality would be affected by the event. There are other quite extraordinary omissions, too. One of these is my name. In every reference to me during the first fifteen years of my life, Mother calls me 'the child'. I am presented not as a person, but as an encumbrance. The reader is not even told where I was staying in Germany when Mother was on her travels, and learns nothing of the family that was looking after me.

Seppl carried on meeting Mother in the hotels and guest houses she stayed in on her travels, and in Miltenberg when she came there to visit me. I never knew when she was coming. She seemed to blow in like the wind, chatter about her adventures and then blow out again – often before I had had a chance to tell her my own news. If she had asked me, I would have told her that my news was good. I was happy in my new home, where I felt settled, secure and loved.

I didn't know it then, but there was a particular reason for the warmth with which Oma and Opa welcomed me. It didn't occur to me to ask why there was an old perambulator and pushchair among all the clutter in the house. I later discovered that Oma and Opa had had a daughter who had died in infancy. They never spoke of her. The room that they gave to me was the room in which she had slept: it immediately adjoined their bedroom. There, above the rows of shelves from which bottled fruit and vegetables looked down on me as I slept, was a framed print of an old verse. It was the first snatch of poetry that I learned by heart: '*Oh! Dass sie ewig grünen bliebe,/Die schöne Zeit der jungen Liebe!*' – 'Oh, may it flourish for ever,/That beautiful time of young love!'

Oma and Opa's love for each other certainly hadn't flourished. Theirs was a marriage of convenience. Oma's first husband had been killed in the war, and she had married Opa because she needed someone to help run the Weyrich family business. They got on, but showed each other little affection. But they each showed lots of affection to me. Oma would often sweep me up in her arms or sit me on her knee. She told me stories, taught me songs, and allowed me to help her when she baked biscuits or cakes. She made sure that I was well fed and in good health. She used herbal cures and folk remedies that sound far-fetched now, but they certainly worked. When I got chilblains in the winter, she would make me run barefoot in the snow and then rub my feet dry, put extra-thick socks on them, and sit me right by the *Kachelofen* until circulation painfully returned. Once, I got a wart, and she went down to the butcher's and bought a pig's gall bladder, rubbed a cloth over it, and then rubbed the cloth over the wart. After two or three such treatments, it dried up and fell off.

Opa's love for me was different, and I learned to love him differently in return. Poor Opa was obviously unhappy and lonely. Nobody ever seemed to talk to him or take him seriously. Whether they treated him like that because he drank, or whether he drank because of the way they treated him, I don't know. When he was sober, he was wonderful company for me. He would brush back his short, grey hair, comb his bristling grey moustache, take up his walking stick and lead me on mushroom-hunting expeditions in the woods. His eyes lit up as he explained to me the names of trees, birds, animals and flowers. When we stopped for lunch at a small inn, and ate a ham omelette followed by home-baked bread and local honey, he would beam at me over the foam on his glass of beer, and the whole world would be at peace. But on days when the henpecking at home got too much for him and he slipped out for consolation at the pub, he would return in a very different frame of mind. I couldn't understand a word he said; he seemed to be a completely different person. Even now, if ever I see a helpless drunk in the street, I am reminded of him. Poor Opa! I think I was his only friend.

Summer turned to autumn – which I now thought of as *Herbst* – and the first day of school was approaching. I was nervous. I knew how painful it was to be pointed out as an outsider and to have no idea of how to join in. At least my clothes no longer marked me out as a foreigner. I had worn out or grown out of the very English-looking jumpers and shorts that Mother had bought for me over a year ago, and Oma had kitted me out in lederhosen, bright braces and stout boots. With my shock of snow-blond hair, I made a convincing little Bavarian – until, of course, I opened my mouth to speak.

At half-past seven one soft September morning, Oma took me by the hand and led me across the Marktplatz and down the lane to the Volksschule. When she left me at the door, I felt physically sick. But when my teacher came over to introduce himself, I knew I was going to be all right. Herr Arnold welcomed me with the kindness that he displayed always and to everybody. '*Grüss Gott!*'* he said, formally, shaking my hand and smiling. Then, in jerky but idiomatic English, he explained that Herr and Frau Sauter had told him all about me, and how pleased he was to have me in his class. I needn't worry about understanding my new language, he explained. If ever I got stuck, I only had to ask. Then he handed me a big, conical bag made of coloured paper tied with a ribbon, led me to my desk and invited me to sit. The place on my right was occupied by a pretty girl with dark hair, who introduced herself as Magda. She had been given a paper bag, too, and had already opened it. It was full of what I now knew were called *Bonbons* – sweets. She offered me one, and I took it. I opened my own goody-bag and offered her one in return.

When all forty desks in the room were occupied, Herr Arnold called us to order and gave us each a *Tafel*, a slate in a wooden frame with a sponge on a string. One side of it was marked with red and white lines, the other was plain. He then handed us all a *Griffel*, a kind of stylus that left white lines on the slate, and showed us how to use it. Before we knew it, it was time for the mid-morning break, in which I ate the sandwich that Oma had so carefully prepared for me. Then the bell rang, we all ran back in to our desks, and the rest of

*The traditional Bavarian Catholic greeting. Its meaning amounts to 'God bless you.'

the morning flew by as we copied letters from the blackboard onto our squeaky, scratchy slates. At twelve-thirty, school ended. The rest of the day was our own.

With Herr Arnold's help, I quickly picked up enough German to join in classroom activities, although I didn't understand a lot of what I was writing down or why. Among the first words I learned to recognise were the titles of the subjects that we studied. *Rechnen* meant counting and working with numbers – I was quite good at that – and in *Geschichte* we were told about exciting things that happened long ago: stories of kings, and knights and battles. In *Erdkunde* we were taught about mountains, rivers, seas and foreign countries. *Singen* was fun, and was easy: I had a good voice, and simply imitated the sounds of the words that I did not understand. I would do so hesitantly at first; then, when I was sure that I had got it right, I would sing out loud and true and be praised for it. *Zeichnen* – drawing – was even better. Language didn't come into it at all. We were given sheets of paper, pens and pencils and shown how to make careful copies of photographs or prints of paintings in books. Occasionally, we were allowed to draw whatever we liked. One of the first things I drew has somehow survived all these years. It's a picture of a train leaving a railway station. One of the figures on the platform is the guard, waving it off. I had been a passenger in such trains many times in the previous year, and my little drawing includes details including benches for waiting passengers, the funnel, dome and whistle of the steam engine, and the coal wagon immediately behind it. In fine weather we would have *Turnen* on the playground. I enjoyed that, too. It was a kind of physical training, in which we stood in lines in blue shorts and white vest to do arm, leg and body exercises to words of command. Even before I understood what those words meant, I could get it right by imitating everybody else.

I was happy. I knew nothing of the daemons that had driven Mother to Germany, or the sexual magnetism that had drawn her to Miltenberg; but however it had happened, I was glad to be there. I no longer saw myself as an irritating aspect of the life of another; now, I was permitted to be a person in my own right. My world was suddenly full of colour – and of people with whom I could relate. Seppl's family made me feel at home not just with them, but with the whole community. They were an important part of it, with their fine shop in the very middle of the town. Everyone knew them – they made sure of it, it was good for business – and everyone knew that they had taken an English boy under their wing. There was no disguising the fact that I was a foreigner – though I was working on that – but during the first year of my schooling under Herr Arnold, I wasn't once made to feel that I didn't belong.

I made friends. The first was the son of a neighbour. Helmuth Blatz's father ran the tourist office that occupied the ground floor of the next-door building, and the family lived over the shop. Tourism was the major local industry – it still is – and Herr Blatz was a local bigwig. Seppl's family encouraged our friendship, and I was happy to follow Helmuth's lead. He had a spinning top that he used to whip along the pavement. I was fascinated by it, and badgered Seppl to buy me one. Helmuth taught me how to make it work. When we got bored with our tops, he showed me how to make a pair of stilts from bits and pieces of timber we begged from the men in our workshop. We made hideouts from branches and fallen leaves in the woods behind the town, and when *Herbst* turned to *Winter*, we tied bits of plank to our boots to make skis. We played ice hockey with old walking sticks and squashed tin cans. Seppl bought me some skates. When *Winter* turned to *Frühling* and the snows melted, we would throw sticks, planks and bottles from the bridge into the River Main that was by then in full flood, and marvel at the power of the water.

Magda was a good friend to me, too, though I only really saw her at school. Her father was another important figure in Miltenberg: he was in charge of the dredgers that kept the river navigable. Magda was as clever as she was pretty, and she would always finish any written task quickly. Then she would look to see if I was struggling – which I often was – and lean over to whisper words of help. Herr Arnold must have noticed, but he never mentioned it. Except once, when Magda dropped her rubber, and she and I both bent down to pick it up. Our heads banged, and Herr Arnold made a comment that made the class laugh, and reduced the two of us to blushes. By then, my German must have been improving, because I remember the words he used precisely: '*Wenn ihr euch lieben wollt, nicht in meiner Klasse, bitte!*' – 'If you two want to love each other, don't do it in my class, please!'

There were less innocent pleasures, too – though I was too young to realise their significance. Sometimes, the town would be alight with excitement as detachments of soldiers marched through, led by a military band. We boys would run along beside them, falling behind as we tried to match the long, stamping strides that crunched through and echoed round the Marktplatz. The thrill of the music was physical. Our bodies buzzed to the tubas, tingled at the glockenspiels, and shook with the thumping of the drums. We cheered, we sang – and we saluted. I learned to shout '*Heil Hitler!*' like the rest. The first Hitler Youth parade I saw electrified me. Seppl lifted me onto his shoulders so I could watch it. Behind fluttering banners, rattling side-drums and blaring bugles, row after row of uniformed boys marched past with jutting chins and jaunty caps. I didn't think of them as boys; to me, they looked like gods. When Seppl told me that one day I might be one of them, I could hardly believe him – it seemed too good to be true.

The grandest parade of the year took place in April, on Hitler's birthday. I experienced this first in 1937. The column that marched through the town seemed endless, and each section was led by its own band. We cheered them all, shouting until we were hoarse. Soldiers marching ten abreast were followed by senior and junior sections of the HJ and its female counterpart, the *Bund Deutscher Mädel*. There was a detachment of the *Arbeits Dienst*, 18- and 19-year-old men conscripted to do public works projects for a year. They weren't armed, but carried polished ceremonial spades. Then came a fleet of long, low, open-top Mercedes staff cars with swastika pennants on the bonnet, and swastika-armbanded guards on the running boards. The symbol was everywhere: on banners hanging from every window in Miltenberg, and on the little flags that we had all been given to wave.

I didn't see those red, black and white flags as symbols of Nazism; I saw them as the symbol of the nation (which indeed they had been since September 1935). Nor did I think of those occasions on which we waved them as political events; to my childish imagination, they seemed like celebrations of life. Germans were rejoicing at being Germans – that was what they did. And that was what I wanted to do, too.

For the time being, I could only enjoy those parades as an onlooker, but there were other ceremonies in which I could play an active part. Seppl's family were not particularly pious, but (like three-quarters of the population of Miltenberg) they were Roman Catholics, and I had been baptised a Catholic, too. Mother had never taken me to church, of course; she had dismissed 'organised religion' as 'unfit' for her and her son in the article she had written for the *Daily Mirror* in 1935. I don't know whether she ever shared such thoughts with Seppl, but she can't have said anything about them to Oma, because every Sunday I would accompany her to mass, and on high days and holidays the rest of the family would come too. Mass in those days wasn't like it is now. The service was in Latin and, except when they were singing hymns, the congregation would stand, sit or kneel in silence, while *Ministranten* – altar servers – would respond to the priest's prayers on their behalf. There was a sense that something very special and very holy was being acted out by the priest and servers in the sacred space behind the altar rails. It wasn't long before the *Ministranten* included me.

My first year of school was a period of almost perfect happiness, but a shadow fell over me on the very first day of the next. It was cast by my new teacher, Herr Göpfert. Squat, piggy-eyed and frequently Party-uniformed, Herr Göpfert's

first words to us were a rebuke. When we stood and said
'*Grüss Gott!*' as we had always done with Herr Arnold, he
waved away our words ill-temperedly and told us that in his
class, the correct greeting was '*Heil Hitler!*' and the Party
salute. He made us do it several times until he was satisfied.
Each day, he would salute back with a swagger, then say '*Setzt
euch!*' ('Sit down!') and '*Tafeln raus!*' ('Get out your slates!').

We all hated and feared Herr Göpfert, and I probably feared
him more than most. His tools as a teacher were corporal
punishment, sarcasm and mockery, and all three were frequently directed at me. I didn't get off to a good start. We
spent much of each morning copying what Herr Göpfert had
written on the blackboard, and he would wash the chalk off
his hands at a washstand in the corner. Every so often, he
would order someone to get rid of the dirty water. It was my
bad luck to be the first one given the job. 'Briscoe, empty the
bowl!' he barked. Too frightened to ask for further explanation, I took him literally, and emptied it straight on the floor.
The rest of the class let out a roar of laughter, but it soon
stopped when they saw the anger on Herr Göpfert's face. My
embarrassment was so great that it has blotted out my
memory of what happened next. He used to keep an empty
desk at the front of the class for boys to bend over while being
beaten with the cane that he kept clipped under his desk. If he
beat me that day, the pain can have been nothing compared to
my shame. He certainly beat me often enough later on.

Like all bullies, once Herr Göpfert found a weakness, he
would work away at it. He took every opportunity to remind
me that I was not German. One of his favourite tricks was to

stop whatever he was saying to the class and ask me to trans-late a particular word into English. Whether or not I knew the answer, the point was made: everyone was reminded that I was a foreigner. If I got it right, I would be praised with sarcasm for knowing the obvious. If I got it wrong, I would be mocked for not knowing my own language. He even turned the only compliment he ever paid me into a put-down. Much of our energies that year were spent in learning to write in Germanic script. We all found it hard to form the letters neatly and accurately, but when we competed for a prize for copying out Hitler's motto, '*Ein Volk, ein Reich, ein Führer*',* my efforts turned out to be the best. When Herr Göpfert held my slate up for the rest of the class to admire, he adopted a look of exaggerated amazement and said, '*Der Paul hat das gemacht . . . ein Engländer!*' ('Paul has done this . . . an Englishman!'). Worse, though, was when he sent me on an April Fool's Day errand to the pharmacist to ask for ten pfennigs' worth of *Ich Weiss Alles* – 'I know it all' – tablets, and primed the class to mock me on my empty-handed return.

Nobody liked Herr Göpfert, not even those who laughed loudest at his cruel jokes. As the summer holidays approached, we were all wishing our last term with him to come to an end. But there was another reason to look forward to the summer. 1937 was the 700th anniversary of the granting of a charter to Miltenberg, and a week-long celebration was to take place at the end of August. Concerts, plays, dances, fireworks, sports displays and military parades were planned, and the whole

*'One people, one empire, one leader!'

town was to be decked out with flowers and flags. One event far exceeded my childish expectations. At two o'clock on Sunday 22 August, there was a re-enactment of the storming of the town by the Swedish king Gustavus Adolphus. There was a magnificent mock battle with troops in period costume, and the streets rang with the shouts of the soldiers, the booming of cannons, the rattle of muskets, and the clatter of horses and wagon wheels on cobblestones. We had a grandstand view from our back garden, and I remember feeling the hairs on the back of my neck bristle with boyish excitement at the smell of gunpowder and the sight of smoke drifting over the rooftops. What a wonderful thing it must be to be a real German! What a glorious thing was war!

*

It is only four o'clock, but it is nearly dark. Outside, the first snow of the season lies on the ground. Downstairs, light is spilling out of the shop into the greyness of the Marktplatz, but through all the other windows dusk is spilling in. I am waiting in the sitting room, watching the outline of the furniture fade, listening to the ticking of the clock. It is 6 December 1937, and I have been promised a visit from St Nicholas. I have been waiting for him all afternoon. The quarter-hour strikes; still he hasn't come.

Then there is a loud knock at the back door, followed by another, and then a third. It sounds as if the noise had been made with the end of a heavy staff. This must surely be St Nicholas – no ordinary visitor would announce his arrival like that. There are two sets of footsteps on the stairs. They are heavy and lumbering, and accompanied by the sound of clanking metal. It has to be them. I know that the saint's servant, Knecht Ruprecht, wears chains around his neck. I know that the saint himself carries a staff. Oma showed me a picture of them when she marked the date of his arrival on the calendar in the kitchen. I have been counting down the days for weeks.

I hear his voice before I see him. It comes booming out from the darkness in the hall. '*Wo ist der Paul?*' ('Where's that Paul?') 'In here!' I reply, surprising myself by the catch in my voice. I have been eagerly looking forward to his arrival, but there is something about his tone that makes me unsure. He is taller than I expected, and unsmiling, which surprises me. His eyebrows are as bushy as his beard. He is wearing a thick red coat and carrying a book that looks like a ledger. He steps into the room, and I catch sight of his servant, who has been hidden behind him. What I see makes me draw my breath in fright.

Knecht Ruprecht looks like a fairy-tale goblin. His clothes, his face and his hands are utterly black. He stands crookedly, writhing and wringing his hands. A heavy chain is draped round his neck.* He is grinning, but the grin isn't friendly. The saint hands him the book, and the servant holds it open for him to read.

'So,' said St Nicholas. 'What do I see? You don't finish the food that is put in front of you. You never wash thoroughly.

*Traditionally Knecht Ruprecht is dressed as a chimney sweep. The chains are used to drop weights down chimneys to displace soot.

You don't pay attention to your homework. You leave your belongings all around the town. Is there anything good you have done?' I am too frightened to think, let alone speak. He turns to Knecht Ruprecht, who produces a coal sack that is as black as he is. The saint nods, and the servant lunges forward, slips it over me, and then picks it up, turning me upside down. The weight of my body forces my face against the hessian and I struggle for breath.

It is only a charade, a well-meant folk custom, but to me, it is terrifyingly real. It is true: I do often leave food uneaten; I hate washing; I haven't really put my heart into my homework; and I have recently lost my schoolbag and a jumper through carelessness. How does St Nicholas know all this? My head spins as Knecht Ruprecht swings the sack over his shoulder and stomps towards the top of the stairs. Then he stops. I push my hands against the sack to hold it away from my face, and whimper a plea to be let out.

'*Ja, lass ihn 'raus!*' ('Yes, let him out!') It is the voice of St Nicholas. Knecht Ruprecht puts me down on my feet and lets the sack fall from around me. 'Will you work hard, be sensible and clean?' says St Nicholas. 'Of course,' I stammer. I would promise the earth to be freed from the choking darkness of that sack. They let me out, but my torment is not over. The saint explains that I have to pay a forfeit for my sins. I have to recite a poem I knew by heart. I can hardly get the words out. I falter, and he takes pity on me at last. 'Ruprecht, give him a *Rute*,' he says. The servant hands me a small broomstick hung with sweets, dried fruits and small toys. I stand there staring at it as they stomp and clank down the stairs and out through the shop. Oma and Opa are in the room, and they are smiling. Why have they let this happen to me? They must see how upset I am but they laugh it off, saying it will do me good. If by 'doing me good' they mean making me feel guilty and terrified, then it has worked.

*

My first Christmas memory is wrapped in a blanket of snow. Christmas 1935 had been snowy, but I hadn't noticed: I had been too ill to get out of bed and look out of my boarding-house window. If it snowed at Christmas 1936, I can't remember it; the season passed quietly and without memorable incident. But December 1937 was different. Christmas is a celebration of home and family, and by then I felt thoroughly at home with a family that I regarded as my own.

I watched the first big, wet flakes fall through the air like feathers. The next morning, everything seemed unusually quiet. I must have woken early, because when I drew back the curtains and wiped away enough condensation from the glass to be able to look out onto the Marktplatz, there wasn't a track or a footstep in the whiteness that filled the square. Beards of ice were hanging from the spouts of the fountain, and the figure that topped its central pillar had been capped with a crazy bonnet of white. The irregular, angular roofscape of Miltenberg looked softened beneath its new-fallen covering; below, the timbering on the tall fronts of the buildings stood out in sharper focus.

The snow stayed. The town sounded different. The clatter

of cartwheels on cobblestones was replaced by the rush of sleighs drawn by steaming horses. Shouted greetings faded before they reached the other side of the street. Booted footsteps crunched and squeaked. Toes, fingers and noses tingled then burned with cold. Life was suddenly full of new sights, sounds and feelings, and I snatched at them all with excitement. As Christmas itself approached, my excitement grew keener. A huge tree was erected and decorated beside the fountain, and no sooner was it up than its branches were hung with snow. Days were short, but when the sun was down, the sky seemed to be lit from below – the glow from street lamps picked out frozen snow crystals and made them sparkle. Then the whole town made its way along swept and gritted pavements to midnight mass.

So many candles were lit in the church that the smell of wax hung in the air. It was soon overpowered by clouds of incense, and so were we. I was the smallest of the *Ministranten*; my role was to hold the boat-shaped container from which the priest spooned incense into the thurible. At the bottom of it was the charcoal that another server had lit in the sacristy and fanned to glowing by swinging the thurible in circles beside him like a cinema cowboy spinning a lasso. Out on the sanctuary, when the gummy crystals touched the whitened charcoal, they hissed as they turned to liquid smoke. Meanwhile, the congregation sang carols that filled the building with joy, and the choir's chants drifted heavenwards through the roof.

After the priest had blessed and dismissed the congregation and we had all processed back to the sacristy, I rushed out and pushed my way through the crowd to join Oma, Opa, Seppl and Maria, who were in the thick of the throng on the church steps. Everybody was shaking everybody else's hand, and wishing one another *Frohe Weinachten*;* my new family seemed to be doing more shaking and greeting than most. I couldn't wait to get home for my presents; I tugged on Oma's coatsleeves until eventually she took me by the hand and we all made our way back across the square. Opa then disappeared into the 'best room' and we all waited for him to ring a little bell to let us know that it was time to enter. When the door was opened, we could see that the candles on the tree had been lit and the figure of the Christ-child was in the crib beneath. Arranged around the tree was a little heap of presents, most of which seemed to be for me: hand-carved wooden toys, picture books, sweets, nuts and home-made biscuits. Suddenly, the long day was over, and I was fast asleep with a copper hot-water bottle in my bed. I have never since enjoyed such a perfect Christmas. At no time in life has my happiness felt so complete. Only now, when I come to write about it, do I realise that there is something about my first real Christmas that I cannot remember. Mother must have spent it with us, surely; but when I picture the smiling faces around the crib and tree, hers is not one of them.

Not all my early religious experiences were as positive. At school, we were taught the faith by one of the older priests who served the parish, a sombre, steel-spectacled figure who travelled about on an overlarge bicycle. He used to mount it by stepping onto one of the two long pins that stuck out of the

*Happy Christmas!

spindle of the rear wheel. People stood back so as not to be clipped by the pins as he passed. But there were other reasons for giving him a wide berth. The joy of Christianity had somehow evaded him, and as he rode about, black soutane fluttering, there was always a sour look on his face. He taught us religious doctrine by rote. If we stumbled in response to a catechism question, he would reach for his cane and use it. But we didn't fear him as we feared Herr Göpfert. We despised him; we thought him weak. Both men taught us that life had to be lived according to a set of rules and principles. Göpfert's made him arrogant and triumphant; Fr Braun's* made him disappointed and sour. Standing up to Göpfert was as pointless as it was unthinkable, but resisting Fr Braun was an art. When we hadn't learned our catechism and there was a chance we would be caught out and beaten, we would take a piece of onion from our lunchbox and rub our hands with it. The point was not to lessen the pain, but to make the fingers swell more, so that when we got home we could show our families that our religious education teacher was a vicious brute.

On one occasion we got much more satisfying revenge than that. Fr Braun was as miserable when he preached as when he taught, and he punctuated his Sunday sermons by banging his fist on the edge of the pulpit. One of my fellow servers saw this as an opportunity to get our own back on him for his sullen lessons at school, and I was invited to join the gang that got to

*I can't actually remember this unpleasant man's name, so I have made one up for him.

church early to put upturned drawing pins under the lace cloth that trimmed the pulpit's edge. Down came the fist, followed by a stifled gasp. He must have guessed it was us, because he spun round instantly in our direction before checking himself and carrying on. We, of course, were sitting with pious eyes fixed on the floor – but when he carried on preaching, we shared a quick and satisfying smirk.

I don't suppose Fr Braun's sourness was caused by the difficulties the church endured under Nazism, but they can't have helped. I knew nothing of such problems at the time, of course: my world contained nothing that I recognised as political. When, in 1937, signs saying '*Hier grüsst man mit "Heil Hitler"*' – 'Here, the greeting used is "*Heil Hitler*"' – started appearing in the shops, I didn't see it as particularly significant. But of course it was. Replacing '*Grüss Gott!*' with '*Heil Hitler!*' was an attempt by shopkeepers to distance themselves from the condemnation of the Nazi regime that had been issued in March by the Pope.* Priests seen as opponents of the government had been rounded up on trumped-up charges of corruption; after the Pope's letter, the number of arrests only increased. Soon, '*Grüss Gott!*' was rarely heard, except at home. In public, people greeted one another not in God's name, but in the name of the Führer. I did the same as everyone else; all I ever really wanted to do was fit in. But I noticed that – for all his faults – Fr Braun never gave the Nazi

*The encyclical letter *Mit Brennender Sorge* ('With Burning Sorrow') complained of Nazi breaches of the concordat signed with the Vatican in 1933.

greeting, or returned it. It was a small sign of resistance, but adults must have recognised its significance.

It was only when I read *Daemons and Magnets* that I learned that a priest who had taught religion to one of the other classes at school had gone so far as to warn Mother of the moral danger in which she had placed me.

A young Catholic priest who taught the children catechism in the *Volksschule* approached me once to sound me out, as discreetly as he could, about my impression of the régime. I sensed the need for caution in his voice and manner, but he did his best to enlighten me, at some risk to himself. I think he was doing it for the child's sake, chiefly, to save him from being indoctrinated in the new Nordic creed, which discounted Christianity as an enfeebling influence on young males. Germans, he said, accepted everything in totality, it was in their nature, and I must remember that. He did not think, he added hopefully, that the English did. He dared say no more.

My life would have turned out very differently if she had listened to him.

4

Mother's New Friends

1937–39

I have, however, occasionally been accused of making allowances for people whose conduct is inexcusable, and so I will simply say that I think there are circumstances and situations which can make saints, heroes, criminals, cowards, lovers of us, given the right moment.

Catherine Dee, *Never Carry the Donkey*

Mother's visits to Miltenberg became less frequent. Her relationship with Seppl was cooling, and there was no more talk of moving in with him for good. There can't have been a big falling-out, because they continued to be friendly, and there was never any suggestion that I might have to leave. They still got on well when Mother visited, but when she wasn't around, Seppl got on well with other women, too. He flattered them, he amused them, he made them feel they were the centre of his attention. Mother was not the only woman to warm to that treatment.

Meanwhile, back in England, she had found another magnet to attract her. Molly Hiscox had invited her to share her flat at 50 Thornton Road, Streatham, where she had introduced her to her lover, Richard Houston, known as 'Jock'. Mother immediately fell under his spell. The fascination wasn't sexual, it was political. Jock, then aged 31, was a fanatical admirer of Hitler and a frenzied activist who fizzed with energy. Fast-talking, short-fused and histrionic, he was a house painter who had – as he frequently reminded people – pulled himself out of the gutter by his bootstraps. But if truth be told, he hadn't pulled himself very far. He was never more at home than when he was standing on an East End pavement on a soapbox, ranting at a crowd in the odd accent of a cockney who had spent much of his life in Glasgow. One of his techniques was to upturn a box on a busy corner and begin a speech to a one-man crowd that was in on the trick. The stooge would heckle, and the dialogue would descend into a shouting match; a crowd would gather, and Jock would have an audience.

Jock told them what he told anyone who would listen: that he, they, and the nation were being kept down by an international conspiracy of Jews. The unemployed were told that the money that should be creating work for them was being hoarded by Jewish financiers, and that their jobs would be stolen from them by 'refu-Jews' from the only country that was dealing with the Jewish menace, Hitler's Germany. Those who had fought in the Great War were told that its only beneficiaries were profiteering Jewish businessmen. And everybody was told that the Jews were cooking up another conflict with Germany to serve their own selfish interests. The problem and its solution were summed up in the slogan chanted by Jock and fellow members of Sir Oswald Mosley's Blackshirts as they marched through the East End of London: *'The Yids! The Yids! We gotta get rid of the Yids!'*

The analysis was crude, hateful and false – but Mother embraced it uncritically. It explained her own failure to flourish: the world had refused to acknowledge her as special because the world was controlled by an elite to which she could never belong. Mother was one of many to find the theory of fascism credible and seductive. It offered dignity to the disappointed, allowing them to see themselves as wronged rather than unlucky or inadequate. Hitler sold these ideas to a Germany that had been humiliated in the recent war; Jock, and others like him, peddled them to Englishmen robbed of jobs and self-respect in the subsequent peace. But there was another reason for Mother's enthusiasm. Jock saw himself as a leading figure in English fascism. He boasted that when England had a Fascist government, he would be a Gauleiter* and his friends would be figures of influence. Mother's admiration for him was genuine, but it was not without self-interest.

If Hitler had won the war, Jock might very well have been given the power he craved, though I wonder how long he would have hung on to it. He was a misfit. His personality wasn't flexible enough to enable him to cooperate with

---

*A Nazi regional controller. Jock used the term loosely; strictly speaking, a Gau was a region of Nazi Germany.

anyone else. He only really got on with two people: Molly, who worshipped him, and Mother, who was then in awe of him. Everybody else he met would sooner or later disagree with something that he said and be dismissed as *'stupitt'*, a word he pronounced often and in the Glaswegian manner. In the early 1930s, Jock had been the blue-eyed boy of Sir Oswald Mosley's British Union of Fascists, drumming up recruits so effectively that he was paid by the party to deliver speeches. In 1936, though, Mosley was attempting to tone down his party's anti-Semitism for tactical reasons, and when it got out that Jock had been fined forty shillings in 1935 for using insulting words and behaviour during one of his soapbox rants, Mosley expelled him from the BUF.

But there were plenty of other pro-Nazi and anti-Semitic organisations willing to give Jock a platform, and Molly and Mother accompanied him to many of the meetings he addressed. What they didn't know was that these meetings were attended by Special Branch officers and MI5 agents, whose reports have since been declassified, as well as by journalists, whose reports were published at the time. One of the meetings Jock harangued was that of the Nordic League, which defined its role as 'exposing and frustrating the Jewish stranglehold on our Nordic realm'. A report in the *Daily Worker* of 22 July 1939 describes what League meetings were like:

> The audience works itself up into a frenzy of anti-Semitism with cries of 'P.J.'* and 'Down with the Jews!' At the end of the

*'Perish Judah!'

meeting, all rise, cry 'The King!' and shoot out their hands in the Nazi salute.*

The League had grown out of the White Knights of Britain, a secret society that based its rituals on the Ku Klux Klan, and whose *raison d'être* was to 'rid the world of the merciless Jewish reign of terror'. Similarly anti-Semitic views were held by members of the Militant Christian Patriots, the National Socialist League, the Link, the Christian Defence Movement, the British People's Party, the National Citizens' Union and the United Ratepayers' Association. Jock, Molly and Mother rubbed shoulders with members of all of them. Groups like these squabbled among themselves and with each other, and their membership shifted and overlapped; but they were united in one all-important sentiment: their hatred of the 'international money power' of the Jews.

That hatred did not spring from nowhere. The Jews were easy to scapegoat with such vehemence because at this time low-grade anti-Semitism was taken for granted. It was a fact of life. One of Sir Oswald Mosley's calmer comments on the subject was that in his youth, 'most of one's friends or relations would not have Jews in their houses'.† That prejudice was probably founded in snobbery – how could a Jew be a member of the English landed, ruling class? – but the same disdain was found in every level of society. Stereotyped Jewish villains figured in low fiction and high poetry alike. Gangs of

*Quoted in *Patriotism Perverted*, Richard Griffiths, Constable, 1998, p. 47.
†Spoken to the Advisory Committee on Internment. (Quoted in *Blackshirt*, Stephen Dorril, Viking Penguin, 2006.)

Bolshevik Jews were beaten by the hero Bulldog Drummond in the novels of 'Sapper'; shifty Semitic figures drift in and out of the detective stories of Agatha Christie; there are anti-Semitic assertions in the poems of T.S. Eliot. Jews were the butt of crude music-hall gags. Anti-Semitism was in the air that everyone breathed, and in the language that everyone spoke. You only have to look at a pre-war English dictionary to see how deeply such negative ideas were entrenched:

> Jew . . . *n.* A Hebrew; an Israelite; *(fig.)* a usurer, extortionate tradesman, moneylender, etc. *v.t. (colloq.)* To get the better of in a bargain, to overreach.*

When the culture treated Jews with so little respect, it was easy for Fascists to blame them for society's ills. But the Fascists did that and more, too. They claimed to have proof of an international Jewish plot to seize control of the whole world. Their evidence was a book that had been published just before the turn of the century, *The Protocols of the Elders of Zion.* It purported to be a record of an international meeting of Jews held in Switzerland in 1897, at which a strategy for achieving Jewish world domination 'by violence and intimidation' had been agreed.

Hitler cited the *Protocols* in his manifesto, *Mein Kampf.* His propaganda minister, Göbbels, had the book translated into several languages and distributed throughout Germany and across the globe. Fascists everywhere referred to it to whip up resistance to the supposed attempt by a race that held no

---

New English Dictionary, Odham's Press, 1932 edition.

allegiance to any nation to rule all the nations of the civilised world. But the book was a malicious forgery – a total fake. It had been revealed as a hoax in an article in *The Times* of 16 August 1921, which had shown that great chunks of it had been lifted verbatim from a work of fiction first published in the middle of the nineteenth century. Hitler dismissed such criticism not on the grounds of scholarship (which he despised), but by appealing to the work's self-evident moral truth:

> ... To what extent the whole existence of this people is based on a continuous lie is shown incomparably by the *Protocols of the Wise Men of Zion*, so infinitely hated by the Jews. They are based on a forgery, the *Frankfurter Zeitung* moans and screams once every week: the best proof that they are authentic. What many Jews may do unconsciously is here consciously exposed. And that is what matters. It is completely indifferent from what Jewish brain these disclosures originate; the important thing is that with positively terrifying certainty they reveal the nature and activity of the Jewish people and expose their inner contexts as well as their ultimate final aims. The best criticism applied to them, however, is reality. Anyone who examines the historical development of the last hundred years from the standpoint of this book will at once understand the screaming of the Jewish press. For once this book has become the common property of a people, the Jewish menace may be considered as broken.*

Mein Kampf (München: Zentralverlag der N.S.D.A.P. Franz Eher Nachf., G.M.B.H., 1935). Volume 1, chapter XI: Nation and Race (pp. 307–8, Manheim translation).

Jock quoted *The Protocols* to East Enders from his soapbox. He told his audience that in the face of the Jewish menace, 'pogroms are not enough'. Since most of England's Jews lived within a mile of the street corner on which he was standing, his speeches often resulted in violence. They were meant to. Jock loved nothing more than whipping up a mob to put the hatred he expressed into action, and a brawl between his supporters and local Jews or anti-Fascists was regarded as a mark of success. After his expulsion from the BUF, he created another audience for himself by founding his own movement, the Nationalist Association, whose gatherings he could address without restraint. In May and June 1939 he spoke in Lincoln's Inn Fields on how the banking system was 'monopolised by Jewish interests' and how the Jews were preparing for a 'war in their favour'. Each lecture was attended by over 700 people. Other speakers at his rallies included J.F. Rushbrook of the Militant Christian Patriots, and Dr Leigh Vaughan-Henry of the National Citizens' Union, who spoke on 14 May against 'international finance and Jewry' at a rally in Trafalgar Square.

Mother formed a particular admiration for Vaughan-Henry, who was the most educated and urbane person she had ever met. Eloquent and softly spoken in German, French and Italian as well as English, he was a poet and a composer, though his poems and compositions had brought him little recognition or fame – and nobody remembers any of them now. Like Mother, he saw himself as a frustrated artist. Fascism gave him a voice. He wrote about national culture for *The Blackshirt* and gave talks about music on German radio.

Anyone less like Jock would be hard to imagine, but they did have three things in common: belief in their own importance, resentment that their talents had been frustrated, and hatred for the race they blamed for their misfortunes. Mother had always had the first two of those characteristics. By the beginning of 1939, she had learned to embrace the third.

To Mother, it seemed that her daemons and magnets had delivered her to the very centre of the stage on which the great political battle of the age was being acted out, and she was determined to play her part with enthusiasm. She no longer saw herself as a mere admirer of fascism: now she was an activist. There was work to be done, and fate had called her to do it. In the summer of 1939 she set off on a European tour that included the Balkans and the Netherlands as well as Germany. This time, she was not trawling for stories but acting as a self-appointed ambassador for English fascism. Her mission did not achieve anything practical, and the characters she visited were minor players that history has hardly recorded. But Mother believed she was engaged in work of great importance, and Vaughan-Henry clearly thought so too, for he wrote letters of introduction for her to contacts in Bucharest, Belgrade, Budapest and Amsterdam. The one that he wrote to Emil Van Loo in the Netherlands* shows how extreme mother's views had become.

This is to introduce you to a journalist friend and author, Mrs. Briscoe . . . I think this would be a good opportunity for her to

*Dated 6 June 1939.

discuss with you your New Economic Order movement in Holland, especially as she is politically well-informed and ties up her interests in contemporary international matters to that in cultural developments, seen as components of the social and political whole. She is quite Jew-wise and aware of much of the machinations which are worked by international finance. You may find her views proceed further in the direction of totalitarianism than your own, as do my own ideas, as you are well aware . . .

In fact, Mother's views proceeded further in the direction of totalitarianism than those of many Fascist activists at home, and her belief in the machinations worked by 'international finance' was just as fervent. The Fascist cause had become an obsession. She thought and talked of little else, and the more she thought and talked, the more extreme her views became. When she was at home, in the flat she shared with Molly, they spoke about politics. When Jock was there – and he frequently was – they listened while he talked. The three of them attended meetings and rallies at which the speeches all carried the same message: that the Jews were parasites who were conspiring to destroy Western civilisation, and that they were engineering a war that must be stopped. The only real variety in the diatribes that they heard or that Jock delivered was in the different terms of abuse directed at the Jews.

It was only a matter of time before Jock, Molly and Mother found themselves rubbing shoulders with the man that the *Daily Worker* called 'Britain's Number One Jew Baiter'. The anti-Semitism of Captain Archibald Maule Ramsay MP verged on insanity. An Old Etonian who had served in the Coldstream Guards during the Great War, Ramsay had been elected Conservative MP for Peebles and South Midlothian in 1931. His early career in the House had been unremarkable, but reports of Republican atrocities in the Spanish Civil War moved him to outrage, and he began to denounce international Communism with increasing fervour. It wasn't long before he had made the connection between Bolshevism and the Jewish money power that was then being peddled by writers like Fr Denis Fahey, whose book *The Mystical Body of Christ in the Modern World** quotes large sections of the *Protocols of the Elders of Zion* uncritically and includes several extracts lifted from the anti-Semitic magazine *The Patriot*. In 1938, Ramsay read Fahey's pamphlet *The Rulers of Russia*, which asserts that 'Bolshevism is really an instrument in the hands of the Jews for the establishment of their future Messianic kingdom'. Ramsay was convinced that 'the Russian and Spanish revolutions, and the subversive societies in Britain, were part and parcel of the one and the same Plan, secretly operated and controlled by World Jewry, exactly on the lines laid down in the *Protocols of the Elders of Zion* . . . These Protocols are no forgery, and I and others could supply evidence to that effect that would convince any impartial tribunal.'†

In May 1939, Ramsay founded a secret society called the Right Club, whose aim was 'to oppose and expose the activities

*Published by Browne and Nolan in 1935. The book has a preface by the Bishop of Waterford and Lismore and carries his imprimatur.
†A.H.M. Ramsay, *The Nameless War*, Britons Publishing Society, 1952.

of Organised Jewry' and 'to avert war,' which he considered to be 'mainly the work of Jewish intrigue centred in New York'. Membership was by invitation. Two hundred and thirty-five subscribed. There was a silver membership badge in the shape of an eagle killing a snake, with the letters 'P.J.' – *Perish Judah!* The social tone of the club was set by extreme right-wing establishment figures. Meetings were chaired by the Duke of Wellington, and aristocratic members included Lord Redesdale, Lord Sempill, the Earl of Galloway, Lord Colum Crichton-Stuart and the Marquess of Graham. Six members were MPs. Others included A.K. Chesterton, who had told the Nordic League that 'the lamp-post' was 'the only way to deal with the Jew', and William Joyce, who would soon become better known as the Nazi broadcaster Lord Haw-Haw. Among the hundred female members was Margaret Bothamley, secretary of the Link, who was also to flee to Germany and broadcast German propaganda. One of her several eccentricities was her claim to have enjoyed a romantic affair with the Führer in her youth. Before she left the country, she regularly hosted parties for Right Club members in her flat at 67 Cromwell Road, Kensington. Similar events were held by Captain Ramsay's wife at 24 Onslow Square.

How Jock fitted in at these grand social gatherings, I can only guess – but then in the parallel aristocracy of anti-Semitism, Jock was the equal of any duke. Small talk was not about the goings-on in society, but of the perfidious plotting of the Jews, and Jock had plenty to say about that. His relationship with the Right Club was perhaps best described by the entry Ramsay made in his membership list. Most were recorded as 'members'; the great and the grand were awarded the rank of Warden or Steward. Jock was listed as a 'Speaker'. He was certainly that.

Late that summer, Mother arrived home from her Continental tour to find the country preparing itself for the war that she and her friends had worked so hard to prevent. As autumn approached, English Fascists found themselves having to choose between their political beliefs and their loyalty to their homeland. Some found it difficult; Molly certainly didn't. On the day before Germany invaded Poland, and three days before the declaration of war, Mother's flatmate wrote and posted the following letter:

15, Thornton Avenue,
London, S.W.2

The Führer and Reichskanzler,   31-8-39
Adolf Hitler,
Reichskanzlei, Berlin.

Dear Herr Hitler,
As an Englishwoman who has very often been to Germany, I wish you to know that I have unlimited trust in you.
                    Yours,
                        Molly Hiscox.

Ramsay was also inspired to put pen to paper. On 4 September, he sat down at a desk in the Commons Library and composed a 'hymn' that made his response to events clear.

Land of dope and Jewry
Land that once was free
All the Jew boys praise thee
Whilst they plunder thee.

Poorer still and poorer
Grow the trueborn sons
Faster still and faster
They're sent to feed the guns.

Land of Jewish finance
Fooled by Jewish lies
In press and books and movies
While our birthright dies.

Longer still and longer
Is the rope they get
But, by the God of battles,
'Twill serve to hang them yet.

5

Acceptance

1938–39

*In Hessen big anti-Semitic demonstrations. The syn-
agogues are burnt down. If only the anger of the people
could now be let loose!*

Joseph Göbbels, diary entry for 9 November 1938

Hildegard arrived in Miltenberg early in 1938. She was young,
lively, hard-working, generous-spirited and pretty – qualities
that inspired Seppl to offer her a job. Whether she was serving
customers, helping in the office or working in the sewing
room, she always had a smile on her face. Her father was a
cobbler; he would sit in the window of the front room of his
cottage in Amorbach, repairing shoes and anything else made
of leather. He was delighted that his daughter had found a
place in such a respectable business. Shop life continued as
normal, but the place now seemed to have a new focus at the
heart of it. Hildegard's cheerfulness made her the centre of
everyone's attention. She was certainly the centre of Seppl's
world.

That March, we heard that our Austrian 'brothers' had come home to the German Fatherland. It all seemed very logical, especially to a family of *Spießbürger* – small-town citizens with a practical way of looking at life. Everyone at Möbelhaus Weyrich received news of the *Anschluss** exactly as the Nazi propaganda machine intended them to. It didn't mean much to me, but I did sense the excitement in the air, the feeling that Miltenberg was not just a German town, but a part of Germany, a nation in which important things were taking place.

A few weeks later, my own horizons were extended when I moved up to a new class housed in an annexe with views over the river valley. My way to school now took me along cobbled paths and steep stone steps under the old town wall, past the *Hexenturm*, the medieval tower where witches had once been held before being burnt, and beside a neglected cemetery. I found it spooky there, and would break into a run so as to get past it as quickly as possible. The headstones had strange writing on them that I couldn't decipher. When I mentioned this to Seppl, he explained that they were the graves of the town's Jews. The reason that the place was so overgrown and neglected was that there weren't many Jews about to look after it. There had been a time when there were quite a few of them in Miltenberg, but now almost all of them had gone. The government didn't want Jews in Germany and had been making things hard for them. They were having a tough time these days, but then they only had themselves to blame.

*The literal meaning of the euphemism used for the occupation of Austria is 'annexation'.

I knew all about the Jews, of course. I knew what they looked like, because there were drawings of them printed in our textbooks. Jewish men were short and fat, with big lips and bigger noses. They were grandly dressed, but their fine clothes made them look ridiculous because they appeared even shorter and fatter. I knew that they were not – and could never be – real Germans, and that they took advantage of the rest of us in order to get rich, which is why those drawings always showed them carrying sacks of money. I don't remember anyone at home or school ever telling me this with any sense of hatred or urgency; it was just one of those things, a matter of fact. Questions in our maths books would run along the following lines: Herr Goldschmied sells a box of socks for 7.50 marks. Frau Schneider sells a similar box for 6.25 marks. How much more profit does Herr Goldschmied make? In the cinema on Saturday mornings, mind, I saw 'information' films that likened Jews to revolting parasites and rats. I wasn't engaged by them. I didn't get excited about what adults called 'the Jewish question'. I didn't know any Jews personally. There weren't any at school. Oma once told me that Mira, the old woman who ran the haberdashery on the other side of the Marktplatz, was a Jewess, but she said this to pass on a fact, not to inspire hate. I never heard anyone at home actively criticise the Jews.

But they didn't actively criticise the way the Jews were treated, either. Since the Nazis that Mother so admired had come to power in 1933, they had made life for the Jews in Germany increasingly difficult. Jews were not allowed to be employed as civil servants of any sort. Marriage and sexual relations between 'Aryans' and Jews were punishable by law. Jews had to register their property so that it could be more easily confiscated: Jewish businesses were compulsorily sold for nominal sums to members of the 'Master Race', and their Jewish employees summarily dismissed. Only a handful of Jewish lawyers were allowed to continue to practise; Jewish doctors were forbidden to treat non-Jews.

But I wasn't thinking much about Jews or Austrians in the spring of 1938. I was preoccupied with a visitor from home. My Aunty Hilda was going into hospital, and Mother had arranged for my cousin Robin to come and stay with us in Miltenberg. I was so proud to be associated with him when he arrived. He was six years older than me: an elegant English public-school boy, tall, with smartly slicked-down black hair, immaculate white flannels and a school blazer. I didn't cut quite the same dash in my lederhosen and sandals without socks, but I was able to show off my knowledge of the nooks and crannies of the shop and the town, and to act as Robin's personal translator. I had a new hero, but Seppl didn't mind, for Robin immediately took my place as Seppl's chief admirer. Seppl bantered with him in his inappropriately confident English, and the three of us went on all sorts of outings and expeditions. There was lots of laughter, I remember, but it all stopped one morning after Robin had been with us for about a fortnight.

A telegram arrived from London: Aunty Hilda hadn't survived her operation. Robin put on as brave a face as he could muster. I didn't see him cry, but he was clearly crushed. I was more upset for him than by the loss of my aunt, whom I hadn't seen since Mother left me in Germany.

Shortly after Robin flew back to London, I was taken on a journey into the very heart of Catholic Germany. On Ascension Day 1938, Hildegard and I joined Miltenberg's annual pilgrimage to the shrine of the Holy Blood at Walldürn. Hildegard had a simple, honest faith; when she spoke of matters of religion, she spoke from the heart. When she sat me down to explain what the pilgrimage was about, I accepted the story as unquestioningly as she told it. The pilgrimage was in honour of a miracle, she explained. Six hundred years ago, a priest at Walldürn had accidentally knocked over the chalice after consecrating the wine during mass. The wine – which had, of course, become the blood of Christ – spilled onto the square of linen on which the chalice sits. When the priest looked at the folded cloth later, he saw that the stain had formed a series of identical images of the head of Christ. When it was displayed to the faithful, many miracles occurred, and pilgrims had been travelling to Walldürn to pray before the images ever since. Hildegard's piety was infectious, and there was something in it that touched my heart. I burned to see the miraculous pictures; it would be just like seeing the real face of Jesus. Hildegard didn't tell me that we would have to walk 13 miles to see them, but if she had told me it was ten times that far, I still would have wanted to go.

I could hardly believe the number of people that had gathered in the Marktplatz that spring morning. Hildegard and I had to push our way through hundreds of people to get into the church. That was full, too, and all I could see when we got in there was the back of the person standing immediately in front of me. My face was almost pressed into the knapsack he was wearing on his back. Far away, at the front, something was being said at the altar, but I couldn't make out any of the words – and then, somehow, the congregation oozed out to merge with the crowd in the marketplace, and we all resolved ourselves into what seemed like an endless procession. Right at the front was a brass band, followed by monks and nuns in habits, families with babies in prams and toddlers on shoulders, dogs on leads, cripples in wheelchairs, more monks, more nuns, seminarians in cassocks and first-aiders carrying boxes marked with red crosses surrounded by white circles. Every hundred yards or so, teams of two or four men would carry a saint's statue or a reliquary on a platform on poles resting on their shoulders. In front of them, *Ministranten* in lacey cottas held tall candles which kept blowing out in the breeze, or swung thuribles long after the charcoal in them had burned out.

The centrepiece of the procession was a great *tableau vivant* of ecclesiastical authority, in which our throned and mitred bishop was borne on a great chair on poles supported by four burly men. Six others struggled to keep a canopy above his head. He seemed to be riding a heavy, loosely jointed animal that nodded and swayed as it lumbered along. Several choirs led the pilgrims behind and in front of them in popular hymns; the tempo and pitch of the singing varied according to the distance of the singers from the middle. At various points, some would be singing the hymn led by the choir long in front of them, while others would be joining in a different one led from behind. It didn't seem to matter. I took my lead from

Hildegard. When I looked up at her she smiled. I don't think I ever saw her look so beautiful.

We weaved and shuffled our way through the town, out through the old gate tower in the walls and up onto the open road. Our great human chain rolled over meadows and through orchards, passing herds of grazing cattle which seemed to find nothing unsettling in our progress through their landscape. When we got up into the hills, I stopped to look back at the seemingly endless procession behind us, winding its way steadily and fervently towards Walldürn. When Hildegard took my hand and we carried on, I felt a happiness that was complete, but I could not understand why. I understand now. I was loved. I was part of a family. I fitted in. If my feet were sore, I didn't notice.

But the sight of the miraculous cloth was a disappointment. When we finally got into the great twin-towered church and joined the queue to file past the relic behind the high altar, I expected to see cripples enter piously on crutches and run out having been miraculously cured. It didn't happen. Not even once. I was on the point of asking Hildegard how this could be, but stopped myself when I saw how happy she looked. If she wasn't disappointed, surely I shouldn't be. And it seems strange, now, to find that while I can visualise Hildegard's face that day perfectly, I can't remember the face on the holy relic at all, try as I might.

I certainly remember the fair we visited afterwards. Walldürn's streets were lined with stalls selling sweets, biscuits, cakes, trinkets and souvenirs – religious and secular. I bought a huge gingerbread heart from a woman who asked me my birthday and wrote it on the biscuit in icing sugar. There were jugglers and jesters, buskers and clowns. The pubs were overflowing with customers, and pilgrims sat on benches outside, airing their feet and swilling beer from steins and great glass mugs. The walk home was more leisurely and less devout. There was little singing, and more chatting than praying. The bishop, though, returned with as much solemnity as he had been carried out. I remember thinking that this wasn't fair on the men that had to carry him – and then wondering whether it was a sin to have such a disrespectful thought.

In the summer of 1938, Maria announced that she was going to marry her loyal suitor, Willi Schwinn, an architect. I was happy for Maria, for she had been good to me. She was the only really educated member of the household, and she encouraged me to be educated, too. Nobody else worried about whether or not I did my homework, but Maria would always check and offer help if I got stuck. I was grateful for her concern, but it was difficult to feel affection for her. She was a hypochondriac, which made her seem selfish. When I look at a photograph of her now, I can hear her say, '*Ach, meine Gesundheit!*' 'Oh, my health!' She moaned about lots of other things, too, and she had a tone of voice that seemed to irritate those around her. I often saw Opa raise his eyebrows behind her back.

On the other hand, the more I saw of Willi, the more I liked him. He was shy, conscientious and honest – unlike Seppl, whose pushy personality impressed me less and less as I grew older. Willi wasn't as good-looking as Seppl: he was short, and had rapidly receding hair. Oma pointed out to me that he was

Evangelisch – a Protestant. She said so with disapproval, but he seemed to me to have more integrity than the nominally Catholic Seppl. In any event, Willi and Maria didn't get married in church, but in a registry office. We all went to Frankfurt for the ceremony. They made their vows not on the Bible, but on a copy of *Mein Kampf*. Maria showed me the *Ahnenpass* that they had had to fill in: a huge form that recorded both their family trees. There hadn't been a Jewish name in four generations, which meant that they were legally entitled to wed.

*

I am sitting on the banks of the River Main, gazing dreamily at my reflection in the deep brown water. Just beyond the shimmering image of my head, my home-made fishing float sways slightly on the surface of the river. There isn't a cloud in the sky, and the sun is warming the back of my neck. An electric-blue dragonfly whirrs up to the float, circles it, then flies off. The air is still and charged with light. Time seems to have stopped. More whirring. It isn't another insect; it is a distant engine. The noise is slowly getting louder. It is coming from the sky. I look up. A huge, cigar-shaped balloon is moving gracefully towards me, following the line of the river. A tiny gondola is slung beneath it. As I stare, the balloon and the gondola grow bigger. It is only about fifty metres up when it passes over me, and I can see faces looking out of the passenger compartment windows. They wave, and I wave back. The sun hurts my eyes; I look down to watch the image of the airship's transit on the water. Its giant tail fins have

Above left: My grandfather, Adolf 'Addy' Davies.

Above right: Matilda (Til) and Lavinia (Lil) Davies, the maiden aunts who acted as mother's surrogate parents.

Right: Mother aged ten, performing on the violin.

Above left: Mother, aged thirty-five.

Above right: Reginald Robert Briscoe, the father I never knew. Mother has written 'Happy with his dogs' on the back of the photograph.

Left: 'Seppl' (Joseph Weyrich), my foster-father, a natural charmer.

Above: Miltenberg: the Marktplatz and fountain.

Right: Aged six: a typically Aryan little boy.

Below left: With Oma in 1937.

Below right: With Oma and Opa in the countryside above Miltenberg.

Above: Mother (*centre*) and Molly (*behind*) at the Pension Weber in Frankfurt, 1936.

Left: Hilda, mother's favourite sister, on a visit to Miltenberg in 1936.

Below: A Zeppelin over Miltenberg (*see page 84*).

Above: A Keller family wedding. Mother is on the left in the floral dress; I am in the front row, second left.

Below right: Hildegard, my 'new mother', 1942.

Below left: Seppl, cousin Robin and me by the River Main.

Above left: Easter 1939: my first Communion. Lina Keller, my sponsor, is on the right; my friend Helmut on the left.

Above right: The poster for *Spiel im Sommerwind*, the 1939 film in which I appeared.

Below: My Hitler Youth membership book; I enrolled just before my tenth birthday.

Above left: John Middleton Murry's Lodge Farm, near the border between Suffolk and Norfolk.

Above right: Some of the Lodge Farm community: Murry is centre of back row; I am far left of the front row, next to Franz, a German prisoner of war. Mother is far right.

Left: Molly and Jock staying at Polstead Hall guesthouse in Suffolk, where I worked, in 1948. They were inseparable.

Below: My wedding to Monica, 28 July 1956.

Above: With mother, Monica and our children, Catherine and Robert, in Bristol, 1962.

Below: Mother at eighty-eight, still fiddling away, in 1987.

great black swastikas on them. They tremble gently as the Zeppelin moves steadily upriver toward its destination.

*

Later that summer, I opened my curtains one morning to see a caravan of unfamiliar cars, trucks and lorries parked in the Marktplatz. Over breakfast, Oma told me they belonged to some people that had arrived in Miltenberg to make a film. I was fascinated. I had never really thought about films being *made*, before; I thought of them only as things to be watched, on Saturday mornings in the town's little cinema on the Mainstrasse. After I had eaten, I rushed downstairs to see what the film-makers were up to, but when I opened the door, I saw only a wall of backs: half the town seemed to have had the same idea. I pushed my way to the front of the crowd and joined the dozen or so other children who had done the same. We were all hugely excited, but nobody was saying anything: I think the crew must have asked the crowd for silence. We watched some men as they set up a huge camera on a tripod, then an actor and an actress appeared from somewhere. They walked across the square and jumped into a beautiful open-top sports car that was standing by the fountain. All the other crew members stood absolutely still. The crowd's silence seemed to intensify, and I held my breath as the camera started to whirr. After what seemed like no time at all, a man shouted a command that I didn't quite catch, but it must have meant that they had finished for the time being, because everybody suddenly relaxed, and several people lit up cigarettes. Conversations broke out among

85

the people behind me, and I looked around to see who was there.

And then I felt a hand on my shoulder. When I turned round to see who it was, I found myself looking up into the face of one of the film-makers I had just been watching at work. 'Young man,' he said, 'how would you like to do a little acting for us?' I didn't know what to say, so I said nothing. The words wouldn't come – in English or in German. Somebody nudged me from behind, and I heard an adult voice say, 'Of course he would – wouldn't you, Paul?' and I found myself being led by the hand to the group of people standing by the camera. '*Prima!*' ('Perfect!') said the man who seemed to be in charge. His colleagues all nodded and agreed. I stood there feeling alone and embarrassed to be the sole centre of atten-tion, but I was soon joined by three or four other children who had been plucked from the crowd, and we all began to feel rather pleased with ourselves. We had no reason to be so proud, of course; we can only have been singled out like that because of what we looked like. Only later did I realise the significance of my own appearance.

The film was called *Spiel im Sommerwind*; the English dubbed version, which was shown in America in the spring of 1939, translated the title as 'Play in the Summer Breezes'. It is the story of a young man who goes on an extended holiday to avoid being introduced to the girl his parents have set him up to marry. He finds a travelling companion through a news-paper advertisement, and after a series of adventures, he falls in love with her – and finds out that she is the very girl he had gone on holiday to avoid. It's a light-hearted romance, and the plot is really an excuse to revel in the beauty of the *Heimat**: the route followed by the young couple takes them through many of the prettiest places in Germany. The whole thing is thoroughly good-natured. The *New York Times*† review suggested that to watch the movie would be a good way to see the 'beauty spots of Germany, without putting much foreign exchange into the treasury of Hitler's Reich'. It praised the film for containing 'plenty of fun' and 'charming scenes along the open road and in the semi-medieval towns'.

Miltenberg was chosen as a location because it was the very model of a German 'semi-medieval town', the essence of the Germany the film celebrates. I was chosen as an extra because I was the very model of Nordic youth with my shock of blond hair, my blue eyes, my lederhosen, my carved horn braces and my tasselled Bavarian socks. Herr von Norman, the film's director, explained what I had to do. It was all very simple. When he said 'go', I had to start chasing another extra round the fountain. He introduced her to me by name, but I am sorry to say that I now can't remember it. She was a girl of about my age with blond plaits and a *Dirndl*,‡ and looked as typically German as I did – though in her case, appearance corresponded to reality. When the adult hero and heroine drove around the corner and stopped to admire the Miltenberg Marktplatz, I had to catch up with my co-star and

*Homeland.
†1 April 1939.
‡The folk costume with a bodiced dress worn by Bavarian girls and women – and by Julie Andrews in the film *The Sound of Music*.

give her a childish kiss. The role earned me five marks, a bar of chocolate, and a mention in the film's credits as the first of the '*Jungen, die um den Brunnen laufen*' – 'youngsters who run around the fountain'.

Now, of course, I can see the irony of it. I, too, was playing in the summer breezes in a picture-postcard Germany untroubled by politics. I knew nothing of the storm that was brewing beyond my cosy Miltenberg horizons and was very soon to break. In the month during which *Spiel in Sommerwind* was being filmed outside Möbelhaus Weyrich, a decree imposed the first name Israel or Sarah on all Jews so that they would be more immediately identifiable, and the main synagogue in Nuremberg was burned down on the orders of the Gauleiter. Munich's biggest synagogue had already been destroyed, in June. Meanwhile, Hitler's plans to gain *Lebensraum* – living space – for Germans were rapidly gaining momentum. At the Munich conference at the end of September, the British prime minister Neville Chamberlain gave in to the Führer's demands for the Sudetenland, a large part of Czechoslovakia. A month later, Himmler* ordered the immediate expulsion of the 17,000 Polish Jews then living in Germany. They were rounded up, put on trains, and dumped on the Polish side of the border. Such matters were way above the innocent head of an eight-year-old, but then something happened that brought political events inescapably close to home.

---

*Head of the SS, the body that was founded as Hitler's personal guard in 1925 and evolved into an elite army within an army, whose responsibilities included the Gestapo and concentration camps.

On 6 November Herschl Grynszpan, the 17-year-old son of one of the Jewish families expelled by Himmler, walked into the German embassy in Paris and sought revenge by shooting the legation secretary, Ernst vom Rath. When vom Rath died of his wounds three days later, the Nazis seized the opportunity to orchestrate a 'spontaneous' outburst of anger against Jews and Jewish property throughout Germany. On what was to become known as *Kristallnacht*, a hundred Jews were murdered and 30,000 sent to concentration camps at Dachau, Buchenwald and Sachsenhausen, where they were enthusiastically humiliated and mistreated. Twenty five million marks' worth of damage was caused to Jewish homes, shops and synagogues; a fifth of that figure was accounted for by broken glass. Some of it lay smashed in the Marktplatz in Miltenberg on the day that I took part in the wrecking of the town's synagogue. On 9 and 10 November 1938, I saw and did things that marked the end of childhood innocence. My own *Spiel im Sommerwind* was over.

*

A couple of months after taking part in *Kristallnacht*, I began preparations for a very different rite of passage. My classmates and I were to make our first confession and Communion the following Easter, and RE lessons at school were given over to preparing for these two great events. I would like to be able to say that they inspired me with a fervent desire to receive Our Lord in the Sacrament, but all I can remember of them is the emphasis on Sin. We were taught about mortal sins, which were so bad that they meant death to our souls and eternal damnation if we died without confessing them. I don't suppose any of us eight-year-olds had committed any, but just to learn of their existence put the fear of God in us. We were taught about venial sins, which were not deadly in themselves, but which could put us in a state of mind in which committing mortal sins became more likely. We were told about 'occasions of sin' – and how to avoid them. We were told about encouraging others to sin – and how that was a sin, too. We were taught how to make an examination of conscience and made to write out lists of the sins that our eight-year-old consciences informed us that we had committed – and then we had to learn those lists by heart so that we wouldn't forget anything when the time came to make our first confession. How many apples had I stolen from the orchard? How hard had I punched or hit anybody? What dirty pictures had I looked at? What rude words had I used? How many times had I done any of these wicked things?

When we were not learning what to feel guilty about in our R.E. lessons, we were learning about things to be proud of in the newsreels we watched on Saturday mornings. In March, we saw footage of German troops marching into Prague to occupy what was left of Czechoslovakia, which was now to be called the Böhmen and Mähren Protectorate. In our geography lessons we were told that the lands had been part of Germany's living space for the last thousand years, and that the occupation was necessary for our national security. A set of commemorative stamps was issued, and we were encouraged to show our support for the Führer by buying them. They cost all my pocket money, but it was worth it.

When I stuck them in my album, I felt proud to have done something so selflessly patriotic and good.

I made my first confession in April. We all queued up to take our turn, kneeling penitently as we waited, with the first person in the queue positioned far enough from the box so as not to be able to hear what was being said by the person before them. The priest sat behind a grille and a curtain so that we couldn't see him, but we knew who he was, and he must have recognised our childish voices. When it was all over and all my life's misdeeds had been laid bare, I was so relieved that I almost fell out of the cubicle. I was left feeling drained, but euphoric; I felt so pure that my feet hardly touched the ground. God only knows what sins I had committed or confessed to; I certainly can't remember any of them now. But I do know that there was one thing I didn't confess, because nothing I had been taught suggested to me that it might have been sinful. I made no mention of my part in wrecking the Miltenberg synagogue. It didn't occur to me for a moment that what I had done there was a matter of personal morality. It hadn't been an individual act – we had all done it. And we had all done it because we had been ordered to do it by those in authority over us, and it was our duty to do as we were told.

I went to bed early that night and prayed myself to sleep so that no wicked thought or deed could stain my well-laundered soul before the moment I received my First Communion the following morning. When I got up, I was thoroughly scrubbed and combed and put into a smart suit with a spotless white shirt. I watched the others eat their breakfast – there was none for me, because in those days, one had to fast from midnight before receiving the sacrament. When I knelt at the altar rail that morning, I leaned back my head, opened my mouth and put out my tongue just as I had been taught, to receive the body, blood, soul and divinity of Our Lord Jesus Christ with a faith and devotion that I have never felt since. I floated back to my pew in a state of perfect happiness.

Mass was followed by a family feast at which I was the guest of honour. I had the first helpings from a huge platter of salads, meat and cheese, all arranged in the shape of a swan. I was made to pose for photographs; I still have the one taken with Tante Lina, who made a huge fuss of me, telling me that I was turning into a proper little German man, and how much I had grown up since she had first seen me. At some point during my special day, Mother appeared – at least, I think she did. Maybe my memory has deceived me. She isn't in any of the photographs that were taken; perhaps she arrived after the camera had been put away. She makes no mention of the event in *Daemons and Magnets.* But it was certainly about that time that she told me she planned to come back to collect me the following July and to take me back to England for good. She seemed to think I would be pleased, but my face must have showed that I wasn't. Life in Germany was exciting; my only memories of England were of babyish games with Beatrice in the park. Still, I wasn't too downcast to learn that I would be returning. Children, after all, have little sense of time, and tomorrow Mother would be gone. Then I could forget about her until her next visit – and that would be months away. She told us that she was busy with her journalism, and had all sorts of meetings to attend and people to interview. She spoke of world events, but I didn't understand their significance; nobody at Möbelhaus Weyrich seemed interested in international developments, so long as they didn't do any harm to the business.

Shortly after Mother left, Seppl told me that he and Hildegard were going to get married. When Maria had married Willi the year before, they had set up their own home in the town, but Hildegard and Seppl were going to carry on living above the shop. I was pleased, because I had become fond of Hildegard, who was kind and trusting, and never patronised me when she spoke to me. She made me feel grown up. I didn't realise it at the time, but I felt protective toward her. I couldn't bear to think that somebody as pretty and gentle as Hildegard might get hurt. What I also didn't realise was that Mother must have been told of the engagement on the day of my First Communion, if not before. The reason I was in Miltenberg in the first place was that Mother had planned to move there and marry Seppl. Now that there was no possibility of this happening, she must have realised that she couldn't very well leave her young cuckoo in the nest that Seppl was making with Hildegard. It can't have been easy for her. Reading *Daemons and Magnets* now makes me wonder whether she wrote her failed relationship with Seppl out of her story because it was too painful to remember. For someone as emotionally crippled as Mother to offer love and then have it rejected must have been doubly hurtful. My guess is that she buried the pain, and buried it deep.

Summer arrived, but there was no sign of Mother. My ninth birthday came and went. Oma and Opa must have

begun to wonder what was happening, but I wasn't bothered:
I was enjoying another perfect Miltenberg summer, roaming
the woods and meadows, playing day-long war games of
ambushes and battles in which my friends and I pretended to
be the proud and brave soldiers we saw every Saturday
morning in the newsreels in the Mainstrasse cinema.

On 1 September those same soldiers marched into Poland.
Two days later, a radio announcement solemnly informed us
that Britain and Germany were at war. It didn't occur to me
for a moment that this put me in any kind of difficulty. The
barriers at the borders had come down, but I was on the right
side of them. I responded to the news of war just as my school-
fellows did – with excitement. The whole town seemed to
share in it. There were soldiers and army vehicles everywhere.
The town hall was turned into a recruiting centre, and eager
young men waited in queues to join up. Seppl left the shop
one morning and came back wearing a field-grey army
uniform. Shortly afterwards he was posted to the front, and
we didn't see him again for months. There were practice air-
raid warnings, and Opa kitted out the cellar as a shelter. A
blackout was introduced and car headlamps were covered,
leaving only a narrow slit to cast light on the road. Everyone
was preparing for a war that we all were certain we would win.
I could hardly wait to play my part by joining the Jungvolk,
the junior section of the Hitler Youth. You had to be ten to
become a member, but my tenth birthday wouldn't be for
ages.

6

The Enemy Within

1939–40

In fact as a secret society the Right Club exhibited farcical rather than sinister aspects.

Richard Thurlow, *Fascism in Britain*[*]

Back in England, Mother's response to the declaration of war was rather different. Her feelings were of anger, disappointment and disgust. She also felt put out. She hadn't been able to get out to collect me because of visa problems, and now that the borders were closed, I was stuck. Most parents would be frantic in such circumstances, but Mother was – well, Mother was different. She makes it clear in *Daemons and Magnets* that she wasn't really worried about me at all:

> I never doubted that I would see the child again, nor feared for his welfare in the enemy's land, but lived on an optimism which was a kind of sixth sense.

*Basil Blackwell, 1987.

She was just as optimistic about the outcome of the war, but not because she expected that Britain was going to win it. She thought that it wouldn't be long before the Führer called a truce and 'the whole silly business' was over. She said as much to anyone she met, including her neighbours in Streatham; when news got out that there were pro-Germans living in the street, there were so many unpleasant scenes that she and Molly had to move to another flat.

Jock's response to the outbreak of hostilities was to increase the number of Nationalist Association meetings in the East End. The meetings were attended by crowds of up to a thousand, before whom he would rail against the 'Jews' War' into which they had been 'dragged'. He didn't tell the crowds he was pro-Nazi, but he was – and so was Leigh Vaughan-Henry, who was equally determined to carry on the struggle in whatever way he could. He asked Mother to help him organise anti-war activities by becoming his secretary. Shortly afterwards, Molly was invited to help, too. Captain Ramsay, however, saw himself as a patriot, and publicly pointed out that one did not have to be pro-Nazi to be anti-Semitic. He later wrote that 'the spirit of the [Right] Club naturally led the younger members to join the Services, wherein they served with distinction on most fronts'. But he also acknowledged that others saw it their duty to 'continue to fight the internal enemy' which was 'no less formidable than the Axis powers'.

Ramsay later claimed to have shut down the Right Club for the war's duration, but it would be more accurate to say that membership quickly fell away, leaving a remnant of active enthusiasts. By the spring of 1940, there were only a handful left – maybe a dozen or so. These included Mother and Molly, who were not formally members of the Club, but their link with Jock put them at the heart of the action – such as it was. They handed out flyers condemning the war as part of an international Jewish plot. They circulated copies of Ramsay's *Land of Dope and Jewry*. They gathered in twos and threes – as many as they could muster – and sat in newsreel cinemas, booing Churchill every time he appeared on the screen.* They printed sticky-backed propaganda posters and sneaked out after dark to press them onto lamp-posts, public noticeboards and telephone boxes. And they started loud anti-war conversations in pubs.

The impact of these amateurish efforts to undermine the war effort was minimal. The only people who seem to have noticed them were MI5 and Special Branch, who were watching the Right Club remnants' every move. Ramsay didn't know it, but one of his leading members, a Miss Marple-like figure known to him as Marjorie Amor,† was in fact an MI5 plant. In February 1940, two more MI5 agents, Hélène de Munck and Joan Miller, signed up. Six months into the Phoney War, the authorities were beginning to take internal dissent seriously.

*In fact, the authorities took audience reactions seriously. A Mass Observation report on the audience response to public figures in 1940 noted: 'Among politicians Churchill still remains easily the most popular. Although only appearing in 14 newsreels, he has been clapped in 11 of them: this makes a percentage of applause of 77 per cent a higher figure than for any other personality or even for any of the services.'
†Her real name was Marjorie Mackie.

One of the first signs of this came on 22 February when Jock was arrested under the 1936 Public Order Act. After denouncing the war in one of his Nationalist Association meetings on Finsbury Pavement, he was picked up and charged with making 'anti-Jewish remarks'. The case came before court a week later, and he was fined 40 shillings and bound over to keep the peace. Ramsay was outraged and asked a question of the Home Secretary in the House, accusing the authorities of pro-Jewish discrimination. Why had the police arrested a man for stating that this was a Jewish financial war, but let a fellow speaker who had referred to it as a 'capitalists' war' go free? It was one of many anti-Semitic interventions Ramsay made in the Commons. Yet it was to be a private effort to strike at his *bête noire* that was to prove his undoing, at the same time setting off a chain of events that put Mother and Molly at the very forefront of what became known as the fifth column – the enemy within.

In March 1940 one of Ramsay's closest Right Club associates, Anna Wolkoff, introduced him to a cipher clerk at the American embassy, Tyler Kent. Wolkoff was the daughter of an admiral who had been an aide-de-camp to the last Tsar of Russia; the family lived in exile in London and had every reason to hate the Bolshevik regime. Her parents now ran the Russian Tea Room in South Kensington. It had become a well-known meeting place for enemies of Communism, and for admirers of Nazi Germany, Communism's sworn enemy. Kent was a regular customer. He confided to Wolkoff that he had hoarded copies of confidential correspondence between Churchill and Roosevelt, in which the pro-war sympathies of the American president were made clear. Kent was an isolationist; he wanted to keep his country out of the war at all costs. When Ramsay and Kent met, they hit it off instantly – not least because they both believed that the people responsible for the war were the Jews.

MI5 had been watching Kent since the previous October, when he had been spotted handing a parcel to a known Gestapo agent in London. They also had their eye on Wolkoff, thanks to Marjorie Amor and Joan Miller. When MI6, the overseas intelligence service, reported that the German ambassador in Rome had seen the correspondence Kent had copied, MI5 decided that Kent had to be rounded up. In the event, they caught Wolkoff first: she asked Joan Miller, whom she trusted completely, to help her get a secret message to William Joyce, Lord Haw-Haw, in Germany. Miller's colleagues in MI5 arranged for it to be sent through the Romanian legation. The message asked Joyce to confirm its safe receipt by making a reference to Thomas Carlyle in one of his broadcasts. When he did so, Wolkoff's treasonable connection to Joyce was beyond doubt.

Tyler Kent's flat in Kensington was raided on 20 May: copies of more than 1,500 classified documents were found. The authorities had the proof they needed that he was a spy. But they also found something that Ramsay had given Kent for safe keeping, believing him to be protected by diplomatic immunity, which, when it came to it, the American ambassador agreed to waive. It was Ramsay's most secret possession: a red leather ledger bound by a brass lock. When the police broke open the lock, they discovered it contained the full list of members of the Right Club. The names were copied out in Ramsay's spidery handwriting. Many of the members were prominent in the British establishment.

At first, MI5 thought they had uncovered a wide network of traitors and spies, but it quickly became clear that most members had been admitted before the outbreak of war, and it was realised that membership in itself was not evidence of treasonable activity or intent. But the capture of Kent and the discovery of Ramsay's 'Red Book' was nevertheless followed by a large number of arrests. The affair prompted the War Cabinet to amend Defence Regulation 18B in order to allow the internment without trial of those who 'sympathized with the system of government of enemy powers'. This effectively meant that the government could lock up whoever it wanted to without having to prove any kind of guilt.

The mood in the country had changed. The Phoney War had come to an end. The front line of a very real war was rapidly getting closer to England. Germany had invaded Denmark and Norway on 9 April 1940. On 10 May, German troops had marched into France, Belgium, Luxembourg and the Netherlands. That day, Churchill had become prime minister. On 15 May, Holland had surrendered. Churchill believed that fifth columnists had hastened that country's defeat, and he didn't want the same thing to happen at home. He told the War Cabinet that he wanted 'enemy aliens and suspect persons' to be put 'behind barbed wire'. The Home Secretary, Sir John Anderson, counselled caution, but when Tyler Kent was caught and Ramsay's 'Red Book' discovered a week later, opposition to Churchill's wishes dissolved.

The majority of those taken into custody in the round-up that began on 23 May 1940 were members of the BUF, including Sir Oswald Mosley and his closest associates. Ramsay and two other Right Club members were rounded up, too, but Jock, the third Right Club member on the list, went on the run. He and Molly fled London on a white tandem. They travelled the country, living as outlaws. They stayed with political friends when they could, and slept in barns or under hedges when they couldn't. When the weather was bad and they couldn't find shelter, Jock would brazenly walk into a rural police station, claim to be travelling about in search of work, and ask whether he and Molly could spend the night in the cells. They were never turned away. Their luck held until the following December, when Jock was recognised and arrested. He spent the rest of the war in an internment camp on the Isle of Man.

But there was no warrant out for Molly, who rejoined her political friends in London – though there weren't many of them left. Most of the men among them, including Leigh Vaughan-Henry, were now locked up.* All that was left of the Right Club was a handful of supporters, two of whom – Mother and Molly – had never been formal members of it. This was the fifth column that government information films and posters warned the public about. If the public had known

---

*Captain Ramsay was the only Member of Parliament to be interned under regulation 18B. He was released in September 1944. The following May, he proposed the motion that Edward I's Statute of Jewry of 1290, which had been repealed in 1846, be reintroduced. He lost his seat in the post-war general election and died in 1955.

how small that column was, they might have wondered why the government was making so much fuss.* Regulation 18B had cleared the streets of almost everyone who might have chosen the path of treachery – and many who would never have dreamed of betraying their country. But a small circle of Fascist fanatics was still at large, and their mood was becoming increasingly treacherous. Mother's 'magnets' had drawn her to the very centre of it.

By the end of 1940, Britain had been mercilessly battered by the enemy. The point at which anyone might try to excuse pro-Nazi thoughts, words and deeds as misplaced idealism was long past. A couple of days after Jock had gone on the run, the British Expeditionary Force had been forced into humiliating retreat from Dunkirk. The newspapers showed photographs of queues of thousands of troops standing up to their shoulders in the shallows, waiting to be rescued. Everyone knew that the war was real, and defeat all too possible. In July, people living in the south-eastern counties of England watched the Battle of Britain being fought in the very skies above their heads. It was obvious that the survival of the nation was at stake. In September, the Blitz began to rain down fire on British towns and cities. Men, women and children sheltering in underground stations or picking their way through the rubble of their homes knew that their country was engaged in a fight to the death.

*The Gaumont propaganda short *You Have Heard of the Fifth Column – You Can Wipe It Out* warned the man in the street to watch out for lights being used for signalling, rumours being spread, photographs being taken, leaflets distributed, German wireless listened to, and so on.

Mother observed all these things, but not as others saw them:

> All I wanted was peace between us. Besotted and blinded, I did
> not care how. From the bed-sitter window I watched the search-
> lights pick out the leaping, plunging planes at their dog-fights,
> while the Battle of Britain raged on . . .
>
> Sometimes I wondered if another raid on Babylon had begun,
> with archangels coming down in flames in the cause of God and
> regeneration. The thing hovered perilously, on those lonely
> nights of fearful watching, between unbearable reality and apoca-
> lyptic horror. My landlord . . . would beat on my door as soon as
> the warning had pierced the summer air, imploring me to take
> cover. I was always the last to obey. I might feel the awe of the
> Apocalypse but [I had] no fear of the fighters in the fiery battle
> above, where none were my enemies.

Mother was certainly 'besotted and blinded', and I can well
believe that she had 'no fear of the fighters in the battle above'.
But to say that she saw neither side in the conflict as her enemy
is simply not true.

7

Taming an Englishman

1939–41

You are flesh of our flesh, blood of our blood, and your young minds are driven by the same spirit that possesses me.

Adolf Hitler, address to the Hitler Youth*

My new nickname was meant kindly, but it still hurt. They started calling me '*der zahme Engländer*' – the tame Englishman. Given that we were at war with England, I suppose it was a compliment of sorts, but I didn't want to be thought of as any kind of Englishman at all. I considered myself German, like everybody else around me, and I certainly looked the part, with my Nordic features, my shock of blond hair and my blue eyes.

My schoolfriends weren't the only ones to find my nationality suddenly significant. Just after the start of the autumn term, a Party official turned up unannounced at the shop, and

*At the Nuremberg rally of 1934.

I was made to sit in the corner of the sitting room while he asked Oma and Hildegard all sorts of questions about me. The most important one seemed to be whether or not I was a Jew. Oma dismissed the suggestion as ridiculous – I was a Catholic: the whole town had seen me make my first Communion last Easter. The man with the silver *Hakenkreuz** in his lapel wasn't impressed and asked me to show my papers. Hildegard explained that they were back in England with my mother, with whom they had lost contact. At this point, the visitor closed his notebook, stood up, offered the Party salute and left. When Hildegard came back after showing him out, she looked worried, and I asked her if they were going to take me away. She gave me a hug and said that they would never let that happen, but we all knew that if they came for me, I would have to go. I didn't dare to think where they might take me, especially if they got it into their heads that I was a Jew.

That night, I hardly slept for worry, but the following morning, Hildegard said that she had thought of an answer to our problem. She and Seppl would formally adopt me, and then nobody could take me away. Why not? They all thought of me as family, anyway – they had done for a long time. It was the obvious thing to do; after all, they all loved me. She would have to get Seppl to sign all the paperwork, of course, but she was sure that when he came back on leave he would agree. Then she hugged me, and I cried tears of relief. But they were tears of joy, too. For the first time in my life, someone had told me I was loved.

*Swastika.

That still left the problem of the papers. Someone suggested asking the Swiss Red Cross to help, and they managed to contact Mother, obtain the necessary documents, and send them on to Miltenberg. It seemed to take for ever, but by the late spring of 1940 it was all settled. I had a real family and a new nationality. I belonged.

The war gave me a perfect opportunity to demonstrate my loyalty to the nation and the family that had accepted me. The most obvious way of helping the war effort was to join the Hitler Youth. I would be eligible for the junior section, the Jungvolk, when I turned ten in July, but I was allowed to sign up early, on Hitler's birthday. I was the proudest boy alive when I first put on my uniform: black shorts, brown shirt, and a scarf fastened round my neck with a leather knot. I made a solemn oath that dedicated the rest of my life to the Führer:

In the presence of this blood banner which represents our Führer, I swear to devote all my energies and my strength to the saviour of our country, Adolf Hitler. I am willing and ready to give up my life for him, so help me God.

I meant it. I would have carved those words in my heart if they had asked me to. I was even prouder when I became a fully qualified *Pimpf* by passing the first test, the *Pimpfenprobe*. To do this I had to run 60 metres in 12 seconds, throw a ball 26 metres and achieve 2¾ metres in a long jump. I had to learn the words of the Hitler Youth Flag song and the Horst Wessel Song. I learned them well; I can remember the *Horst-Wessel-Lied* even now:

Die Fahne hoch die Reihen fest geschlossen
S.A. marschiert mit ruhig festem Schritt
Kam'raden die Rotfront und Reaktion erschossen
*Marschier'n im Geist in unsern Reihen mit!**

The tune used to make the hairs stand up on the back of my neck. I am sorry to say that it still does.

Passing the *Pimpfenprobe* entitled me to carry a *Fahrtenmesser*, a bayonetlike dagger with a swastika set in a lozenge in the handle. We used it for whittling sticks and cutting string, but it was clearly designed as a weapon. It sat in a metal sheath that we hung from our belts. Wearing it made us feel armed.

Gaining a new nationality brought me a new enemy, and I was keen to show myself to be as anti-British as the rest. One of the ways I did this was to buy the album for a cigarette card collection called *Raubstaat England* – Robber State England – which celebrated the wickedness of the British Empire. It wasn't a very subtle piece of propaganda. On the cover, under the royal coat of arms, was a picture of a huge, clawed hand grasping the globe. I pestered every adult I met for the cards I needed to stick in it. They all showed scenes of British colonists acting with greed, brutality and cowardice. A lot of them were imagined scenes from the Boer War. One that particularly caught my imagination was of a bare-breasted black woman tied to the front of a steam engine so that two English soldiers could hide behind, using her as a shield. Other cards

*'Flag high, ranks closed,/The S.A. marches with silent, firm steps/Comrades shot by the Red Front and Reaction/March in spirit with us in our ranks!'

showed prisoners tearing at the wires that surrounded their concentration camps. The irony of this entirely escaped me. We knew there were camps in our own country, but they were for people that deserved to be in them. We didn't know or choose to imagine what went on in them, but it couldn't be as inhumane as in those that had been run by the English.

I didn't know I was being indoctrinated. I was ten years old. I wasn't outraged to discover that the English were robbers and land-grabbers; I just accepted it as a historical fact. My real interest was in getting hold of the pictures I needed to complete my collection. I would have taken almost as much pleasure in cards of film stars. The fact that the *Raubstaat England* cards showed thrilling scenes of barbarity was a bonus. I carried out a few acts of lesser cruelty myself. With all the men being away in the army, we youngsters got it into our heads that we could more or less do what we liked. We would ring doorbells and run away before they were answered. We would snowball people, especially those that could not retaliate – and if we thought they might be Jewish, we really went to town.

One bit of boyish mischief that got out of hand happened during the 1941 summer holidays. I was hanging around with several other boys of the town, and we were bored. Someone suggested a sword fight, and we headed off to the woods to find some sticks. On the way, we noticed that the pointed slats on an old fence behind the castle wall would make perfect sword blades, and we started to pull the fence apart. The old woman that owned the fence saw what we were doing, and when she screamed at us to stop, we all ran off – but she recognised me by my mop of straw-blond hair, and called to me by name. When I sheepishly crept back, she took me by the ear, twisted it and dragged me back to her house, where she phoned the police. The policeman was a short, grumpy man with a handgun on his belt. When he marched me off to the police station, I stared at the ground so as not to meet the eyes of anyone we passed. When we got there, he sat down at a table and got out a notebook and a pencil and asked me which other boys had been involved. His hand was poised ready to write out a list of names, but I didn't give him any, so he took me down a flight of stone steps, put me in a large, windowless cell and locked the door behind me. I wept. A couple of hours later he asked me if I had changed my mind, but I hadn't – so he took me home and told Oma and Opa what I had done. They were furious. I had brought shame on the family and damaged the reputation of the shop. It fell to Opa to administer my punishment: he beat me pretty fiercely with a stick. What would the customers think when they found out that there was a vandal in the family? I was sent to my room without food for the rest of the day, but when I appeared the next morning for breakfast, nothing more was said.

The only other time that Opa laid hands on me was far more frightening. I hadn't cleared my plate at supper. Oma ordered me to finish my potatoes, and I refused. She flung an accusing look at Opa, and he snapped. He got up, seized me by the throat and pinned me to the floor with one hand, while he reached up to grab what I hadn't eaten with the other. He then knelt on my chest – I thought I would suffocate – and forced my jaws open so that he could stuff the potatoes into my mouth – I thought I would choke. He then hauled me to my feet and threw me to the door. I ran to my room. I stood there shaking with fright, listening to angry shouts from the sitting room. Then there was a silence, and a knocking at my door. I was too frightened to reply. The door opened slowly. It was Opa. He put his arms round me and gave me a hug. He smelled of schnapps. As he moved towards the door he turned round as if to speak, but no words came.

*

Now that Willi had been called up, Maria had moved back to live above the shop, and she, Hildegard and Oma began to refer to me as the man of the house. This made me feel proud; it wasn't very flattering to Opa, but he didn't complain – in fact, he didn't seem to notice. I still loved him, but I no longer really looked up to him. My admiration for Seppl had waned, too. I had a new hero. When Willi came home on leave just after the fall of Paris in June 1940, he brought with him some wonderful news: he had been chosen to design a gun emplacement for the top of the Eiffel Tower. We had all just seen the newsreel footage of our troops marching down the Champs-Élysées, so everybody knew what an extraordinary structure it was. As I watched him working on his drawings at the dining table, I felt myself glowing with admiration and pride. I could hardly believe that he had been given such an important task. It made me want to become an architect, too. But there was something else that made Willi worthy of admiration. He was utterly and straightforwardly honest, completely without side or selfishness. Whereas I had begun to realise that Seppl was a chancer, who would turn any encounter into an opportunity to make a profit. When he came home on leave, he would open up his kitbag and all sorts of goodies would be produced – bottles of cognac, chocolate, watches . . . Willi always came home empty-handed, and Maria scolded him for it. And he always returned to duty on time, while Seppl somehow managed to wangle an extra couple of days.

When these two very different men were away fighting for the Fatherland, their wives would wait anxiously for their letters. When a letter arrived, we would all gather round the table and Hildegard or Maria would read bits of them out. Often, when nothing came for a while, Oma would ask them to reread letters we had heard before. She said it was comforting to imagine their voices speaking the words they wrote. I got no such consolation from the handful of letters I received from Mother. I hadn't seen her for two years, and I couldn't remember what her voice sounded like. In any case, the messages she sent were so short as to amount to next to nothing. They had to be. They came on official Red Cross letter forms, on which she was only allowed to write 25 words. I was allowed to write the same number of words in reply on the reverse. I struggled to fill up the space. It was like writing to a stranger. When the letters stopped coming in the summer of 1941, all thoughts of Mother faded quickly away.

Willi and Seppl's letters were different. They were full of chatty anecdotes, though they said little of any military significance; the censors would have taken care of that. We got our real news of the war's progress from the wireless and from newsreels in the cinema. At first, all the news was good. There were glorious victories in Denmark, Norway, Holland, Belgium and France. Radio reports of these were always followed by the playing of the *Englandlied* – the England Song, which I had learned in the HJ. It was one of my favourites: singing that I would 'march against England' gave me particular satisfaction. The announcements themselves always ended with a '*Heil Hitler!*' It was made perfectly clear to us that the triumphs we were celebrating were the result of one man's visionary genius. Nobody at Möbelhaus Weyrich was a Party member or a Hitler fanatic, but we were as proud as everyone else that Germany was so obviously winning the war. When it was over, Seppl and Willi would return to a land of peace and prosperity. The dark forces that had conspired to humiliate our country would have been smashed. We had been told that one of the darkest of those forces was Communism, and when our troops invaded Russia in June 1941, victories on that front were reported, too. We saw pictures of smiling soldiers racing across huge landscapes in tanks and troop carriers leaving clouds of summer dust behind them. What we weren't told was that before that dust could settle, follow-up *Sonderkommando* units from the SS were rounding up all the Jews and Communist officials they could find and shooting them in the back of the head.

In September 1941 I moved up to my secondary school, the Karl Ernst Gymnasium in Amorbach. This was quite an adventure; it was about eleven miles away, and the only way of getting there was by steam train. The railway line ran through the most beautiful countryside, through flower-speckled meadows and waving cornfields, past apple and cherry orchards, along and over streams, beside the great forest of the Odenwald. When the engine slowed down at level crossings, we Miltenberg boys would lean out of the windows and shout at the girls cycling to school, or wave at the old men driving bullock carts with swaying loads of hay or beet.

Amorbach was a pretty village on the vast estate owned by the Fürst* of Leiningen, which included the huge forests that swept down to the banks of the river Neckar and Heidelberg. The prince's stables and stud farm were at the back of the school, and his palace and park were on the other side of the village. One of his daughters, Kira, was in my class; I knew her because she used to come into the shop with her mother.† Whenever they turned up, everyone fell over themselves to welcome such grand customers. Maria told me proudly that the Fürst's family were related to half the royal families of Europe. For all that, Kira didn't conduct herself with any airs and graces, and she was a good friend of Magda, who had looked after me in my first hesitant days at the Miltenberg Volksschule. I was long past needing help like that when I started at the Gymnasium. I knew most of the people in my class. There weren't many – only fifty or so children attended the school.

By then, I could speak German almost perfectly, and I no longer felt lost or like an outsider. But I still had a significant difficulty. The Gymnasium followed the traditional German

*Prince.
†Her mother was the Grand Duchess Maria of Russia, a descendant of our own Queen Victoria. When she grew up she married Prince Andrej of Yugoslavia.

grammar-school curriculum, which meant that I had to study Latin, which was new to me, and English, which I had so anxiously unlearned. I was the despair of the poor English teacher, who was one of several nuns drafted in to replace the school's regular teachers who had been called up on active service. When she asked me questions in simple English, I pretended not to understand. When she made us repeat phrases by rote, I mispronounced them on purpose. At first, she expressed surprise that an English-born boy couldn't speak his own language, but after a short while, my tactics worked, and she left me alone.

Another reason why I was so keen not to be thought English was that earlier in the year I had seen a film at the Miltenberg cinema that made me thoroughly ashamed of the country of my birth. *Ohm Krüger* – 'Uncle Krüger' – tells the story of the Boer War, which the British started in order to get their hands on the settlers' gold. There were several images that I just couldn't get out of my head. I can remember them just as vividly now. There is a massacre of Boer women and children in a concentration camp. They are murdered because they rise up, outraged, after the Boer leader Krüger's son is hanged and his wife is forced to watch. The gallows are on a hill, and the camera draws back to show a picture just like the Crucifixion. Other images come rushing back. The concentration camp commandant is the young Winston Churchill. In one scene, he feeds fine cuts of meat to his pet bulldog, while the women and children prisoners are forced to eat rations that are rotten. When they protest, Churchill shoots down their ringleader in cold blood. The British players are not only cruel, they are also hypocrites. In one scene, two Anglican missionaries distribute rifles along with bibles in a church with a Union Flag over the cross on the altar. In another, Queen Victoria is shown as a drunk. She has none of the moral qualities of old man Krüger, who was a father to his nation, just like our own Führer.

Yes, I can see now that it was all cleverly distorted propaganda. But when I first saw it I was eleven, and I was utterly convinced. It was unthinkable that our people could conduct themselves with the cruelty of the British. I did not hear the words Auschwitz, Belsen or Buchenwald until after the war. But I did see some people wearing yellow Stars of David in Miltenberg that autumn. When I asked Oma what it meant, she explained that they had to wear them because they were Jews.

8

'One of Us'

1940–41

People like Captain Ramsay, who take a violent line on any particular subject, are, unfortunately, liable to have cranks, 'wrong 'uns', or people with an axe to grind running after them . . .

St John Field, KC*

In May 1940, an anonymous letter was delivered to Scotland Yard:

> Please investigate the right of a certain Mrs Briscoe to be in the Ministry of Information office. This woman has always been a Nazi propagandist, has a large circle of German friends and is to the best of my knowledge married to a German. She has a son by her first husband being educated as a German in Germany.

*Field represented Ramsay during the trial in which he sued the *New York Times* for libel in 1941. The paper printed reports that he had passed to the Germans 'treasonable information' given to him by Tyler Kent. Ramsay won the legal argument, but was awarded damages of only a farthing.

I'm sorry I cannot sign my name as I'm afraid she may do some harm to my friends.

The writer clearly didn't know Mother well. She wasn't working in the Ministry of Information; she was a temporary typist in the Brixton office of the Ministry of Food. Nor was she 'married to a German'. But if a relative stranger could describe her as a 'Nazi propagandist', Mother can't have been keeping her political opinions to herself. In fact, Special Branch had been watching her for some time, on account of her friendship with Molly and Jock. They knew that Mother was a friend of the 'notorious pro-Nazi' Leigh Vaughan-Henry and that she had worked for him for a while as his secretary. They shared this and all the other information in their growing Briscoe file with MI5, which was also keeping Mother and Molly under surveillance.

Mother had no idea she was being watched and was completely unaware that her circle of friends contained government agents masquerading as fifth columnists. When Jock and Molly went on the run in late May 1940, Mother quit her temporary job in London and went to stay in the country, where she thought she would be safely out of sight of the authorities. But this wasn't the case; far from it. Unnamed agents' reports dated December 1940 state that Mother had 'finished her "propaganda novel"' – whatever that was* – and that she was 'quite mesmerised by Hitler'. She also told the

---

*I have found nothing that could be called a 'propaganda novel' among Mother's papers.

agent that her 'great desire' was to be reunited with me, 'but she does not want him to be sent to her, as she wants to live in Germany for keeps'. The report concludes that Mother was 'harmless where she is now at Flowers Farm, Minety', and MI5 asked Special Branch not to make direct enquiries of her for fear of compromising the identity of their agent. But Mother wasn't going to be at Flowers Farm, Minety for much longer, and she certainly had no intention of remaining 'harmless'.

Early in the new year, Mother returned to Streatham and applied for a typing job at the Ministry of Supply. She was appointed on 20 January 1941. Eleven days later, her new employers wrote to MI5 to check that there was nothing on record to suggest Norah Briscoe might be a security risk. They replied that her appointment would be 'undesirable' because of her 'known German and Fascist associations'. But by then Mother had already started work in the general typing pool, and in the bureaucratic chaos that characterised the war, the incriminating letter was either lost, or filed without being read. It was a fateful mistake that allowed events to unfold quickly. On 19 February she was promoted to the Central Priority Department. 'Central Priority' was an arm of the Production Executive of the War Cabinet. Most of its work was confidential; much of it was secret.

Mother told Molly about her new job immediately. Molly invited Mother to come over and talk about it. There was something important that she wanted to discuss. Mother went to see her on Friday 7 March. Just after she arrived, there was another knock at the door, and Molly showed in a man in his twenties who was known to her as John.*

'I didn't know you were expecting visitors,' remarked Mother and laughed. 'I hope he's not a government spy!'

But he was exactly that – and he later wrote a word-for-word account of their conversation, which is now in the Public Record Office. Unknown to Molly or to any of her associates in the Right Club, John had been working for MI5 since 1936.

John opened the conversation by pointing out that Mother and he had something in common. 'I believe we both have relations living in Germany,' he said.

Mother produced a packet of photographs, including one of me wearing lederhosen when I was six. I still have that picture today; it appears here in the plate section. While John was admiring them, there was another knock at the door, and Molly showed in another of her political friends, Mary Stanford,† who had just been released after a successful appeal against her internment under 18B. Mary and John had already met.

Mary enquired how my mother's job was going.

'It's more than interesting,' replied Mother.

*In all the official records of the case, this character is described only as 'Agent Q', who Richard Thurlow, in *Fascism in Britain* (Blackwell, 1987), says 'may have been Taylor', a known MI5 agent. Another suggestion is that Q might have been Ferdinand Mayer-Horckel, the German-Jewish refugee known as Ferdy Mayne, then working for MI5 and later to become a prolific film and television actor. But this is impossible because Q claims to be 'a British subject by birth and parentage' in his witness statement.
†Mary Stanford was usually known as 'Molly', but I call her 'Mary' here to avoid confusion with Molly Hiscox.

'Oh?' interjected John. 'Where do you work?'

'I'm at the Ministry of Supply,' Mother replied. 'Though a better name for it would be the Ministry of Muddle.' The fact that Mother had been employed there despite MI5's warning letter suggests she was right. 'I have just been transferred to a special department, where I get sight of all sorts of important official documents.'

'What sort of documents?' asked John.

'Letters – about a submarine base in Scotland, about short-ages of supplies for factories, materials sent to Ireland and the Near East. When I come across a really hot one, I make a special carbon copy and keep it in a folder in my desk.' It was an astonishingly naive admission to make to a man she had only just met.

'Isn't that just a bit silly?' said Molly. 'Someone's bound to find them. You ought to memorise them – and destroy those copies as soon as possible.'

'Well, I will if you think it best,' replied Mother. 'But I really don't think there is any danger, because no one would ever suspect *me*!'

The irony of that remark now seems pitiful.

'How are we going to get the stuff over to the other side?' asked Mary.

Molly Hiscox suggested they might ask a friend called Teresa Shaw, who had contacts at the Spanish embassy, but Mary Stanford dismissed her as unreliable, and nobody could think of anyone else. So they decided that the problem of how to get Mother's gleanings to the Germans would have to wait. Meanwhile, they agreed to meet again when Mother had a particularly important document, so that they could all memorise it for future use.

That night, 'John' duly reported all this to MI5. It was clear that their watch-and-wait tactics were about to pay off. They had given Mother the rope she needed to hang herself; all that remained was for her to tie the noose.

The group met again that Sunday, this time at Mary Stanford's room at 45 Queen's Gate Terrace. Mother removed two sheets of paper from her bag and passed them around. One was a record of a meeting held at the Ministry of Supply on 13 February about the shortage of spare parts for vehicles bought in the USA and Canada; the other was a letter discussing the possibility of obtaining lorries for the Air Ministry from Southern Ireland. 'This isn't the most important stuff,' she informed John. Indeed it was not. 'But it will give you an idea of the sort of stuff I can get hold of.'

Three days later, on Wednesday 12 March, John telephoned Molly Hiscox. 'Do you remember those curtains your friend had the other evening?' he said. 'I think I have a friend who would be interested in buying them. As this is a private deal, of course, I can't tell you his name over the telephone.'

Molly caught on immediately. 'Excellent!' she said. 'Bring him along this afternoon, if you can.'

John arrived at 60 Stanhope Gardens at three o'clock that afternoon with a German called Harald Kurtz, though he didn't introduce the 'friend' to Molly by name.

She greeted him warmly. 'It's wonderful to meet someone from the other side!' she said. Kurtz was indeed 'from the other side', but not in the sense that Molly Hiscox meant.

He had been working for MI5 since May 1938.* Kurtz and Molly exchanged a few words in German, which John did not understand. John then assured Molly that Kurtz could be trusted, but she seemed to have already decided that for herself.

'I've spoken to my friend about Norah,' said John. 'I told him that she may be able to give him some good stuff.'

'Yes,' replied Molly. 'My friend works in the Ministry of Supply, you know, and she gets valuable information and copies of documents. She brought some along last Sunday, but we told her not to bring out any more in black and white, because it's too dangerous. The trouble is we don't know what is valuable and what isn't.'

'I could probably tell you whether any particular document is useful or not,' replied Kurtz.

'Excellent,' replied Molly. 'I suppose that means Norah will have to memorise it all.'

'I would much rather see the documents,' said Kurtz. 'It would be better to have something in writing – to satisfy my superiors.' That much, at least, was true.

Molly enquired whether it had to be on Ministry of Supply notepaper. What Norah had produced earlier had been her own copies on plain paper. Smuggling out the originals would

---

*Kurtz was an alcoholic homosexual who wanted to become British, which made him easily manipulated by MI5. Graham Greene chose the name Kurtz for the villain in his screenplay for the film *The Third Man* because Harald Kurtz had denounced his cousin Ben Greene as a Fascist sympathiser, resulting in his imprisonment under 18B. Ben Greene appealed and was later vindicated and released.

be more dangerous. John instantly realised this, perhaps sensing that Kurtz was pushing Molly too far.

'Isn't that a bit risky?' he interrupted. But he'd under-estimated Molly Hiscox's anxiety to please. She believed she was talking to a German secret agent. She would tell Mother that memorised or transcribed information wasn't good enough, and that she would have to hand over the documents themselves.

They agreed to meet the following Saturday, the fifteenth of March, at Swan Court, Chelsea, a block of flats just off the King's Road, where Kurtz claimed to live. Molly would bring Mother, and Mother would bring the documents that he would funnel to Germany. They decided that there would be no need for John to come, though he said he didn't like leaving the business to Kurtz and 'the two girls'.

'Don't worry,' said Molly. 'If we're caught, we'll only get ten or twenty years. But you men would have your heads chopped off!'

Molly Hiscox was wrong on both counts; by this stage, it wasn't a matter of if, but of when. She and Mother were now in clear breach of the 1940 Treachery Act, which had been passed to deal ruthlessly with crimes just like theirs. The penalty for offending against it was fixed, and it was not imprisonment:

> If, with intent to help the enemy, any person does, or attempts
> or conspires with any other person to do any act which is
> designed or likely to give assistance to the naval, military or air
> operations of the enemy, to impede such operations of His

Majesty's forces, or to endanger life, he shall be guilty of felony and shall on conviction suffer death.

Mother and Molly were playing with fire, but they didn't seem to have any real sense of the risks. The worst that could happen to political heavyweights like Mosley, ideological extremists like Ramsay or rabble-rousers like Jock Houston was that they would have to sit out the war in internment camps or prisons, but my mother and Molly Hiscox weren't playing politics. They were plotting treason. And now that the big fish were out of the way, MI5 could afford to concentrate on catching the treacherous small fry that remained.

On 13 March, Guy Liddell, director of counter-espionage at MI5, had made the first of several mentions of my mother in his diary:

> The Nora [sic] Briscoe case is developing. M is introducing a German agent and there is to be a meeting when he will get the documents. This case was first brought to my notice on Saturday. One of M's agents was asked to tea with Molly Hiscox, where he met Nora Briscoe, who is the wife or mistress of Jock Houston, the interned member of the BUF. Briscoe said that she was working in quite an important section of the Ministry of Supply and that she had been copying all documents which she thought would be of interest. She is of German origin and has a son who is being brought up in Germany. She is now looking for some means of getting the documents through to the Germans.

Liddell clearly hadn't quite taken in what he had been told: Jock Houston was Molly's boyfriend, of course, not Mother's;

Mother wasn't 'of German origin'; and Jock had long since been drummed out of the BUF. But Liddell had obviously been briefed in some detail on the past week's events, and 'M' clearly regarded Mother's case as serious.

'M' was Major Charles Henry Maxwell Knight, head of MI5's counter-subversion unit B5(b). Knight had been recruited by MI5 in 1925, when he had been Director of Intelligence for the British Fascists. He knew the Fascist mindset, and pursued those with whom he had once shared it with all the zeal of a convert – though he never seems to have shed his distaste for Jews. He was a character of quite extraordinary energy and individuality. He was a crack shot and an expert horseman; he was also an accomplished clarinettist and had played the drums in a jazz band. He was the author of two published novels. He was a Fellow of the Royal Zoological Society; he kept snakes and a bush baby as pets, and allowed them the run of his house. He was an expert in the occult and an admirer of Aleister Crowley. He smoked long, hand-made cigarettes, affected a stylish shabbiness, and surrounded himself with agents who shared his interests. One of his recruits was the author Ian Fleming, whose fictional character 'M' was at least partly based on Knight.

This, then, was the man who had decided to eliminate the threat to the state posed by a shorthand typist and an unemployed tour guide. The two women didn't stand a chance.

Knight arranged for a microphone to be installed in the sitting room of the Swan Court flat. In the early afternoon of Saturday 15 March, he and two members of Special Branch –

Inspector Jones and Detective Sergeant Farnes – tested the apparatus and took up position in the kitchen. They put on their headphones, and Farnes prepared to take shorthand notes of what they heard from behind the locked kitchen door.

At three o'clock Mother and Molly met Kurtz in the entrance hall of the north wing of Swan Court. The place was eerily deserted. The borough of Chelsea had taken a terrible battering during the Blitz, and more than two-thirds of its population had fled. Swan Court was one of many blocks of flats that had been left largely unoccupied. Taking the lift to the fourth floor, Kurtz led the two women down a drab, silent passage to number 74. He showed them into the sitting room, and invited them to sit. The furnishings were shabby and impersonal. An experienced spy would surely have spotted the absence of any sign that Kurtz had been genuinely living there, but neither woman seemed to notice. What follows is from Sergeant Farnes's transcript of their meeting.

'Have you seen the bomb crater at Bank?' Molly asked Kurtz. 'Isn't it just *marvellous*?'

The 100-by-120-foot hole was certainly remarkable, but only someone whose heart had been frozen by fanaticism could have described it as 'marvellous'. It had been caused by a bomb that had fallen on the night of 11 January. The road had collapsed onto the Underground station beneath; the blast had funnelled down the escalator, hurling passengers into the path of an incoming train. Fifty-six lives had been lost. Sixty-nine people had been injured by the blast, the storm of broken glass, or both.

'John tells me you have a son in Germany,' Kurtz said, changing the subject.

'Yes,' replied my mother.

'Whereabouts?'

'Miltenberg.'

'I know Miltenberg very well – I was brought up near there,' said Kurtz. 'Did you know Germany before the Nazi regime?' he asked. Mother said she did not. 'Do you know Berlin?'

'Yes. I don't like Berlin.'

'I'm not very fond of it myself,' Kurtz continued. 'It was absolutely *impossible* to go to Berlin before, because the town was run by *Jews*.' He knew exactly which buttons to press.

'Was it worse than here?' Mother asked.

'Worse.'

'It's bad enough here, good gracious!' interjected Molly Hiscox.

'Of course, you people have been to Germany more recently than I have,' replied Kurtz. 'I couldn't go back after Munich – it would have made me too . . . *conspicuous*.'

'Poor thing!' said my mother. 'It's terrible to have to stick in England, and much worse for you than for us.'

'Yes, but I am doing it in a good cause,' he replied.

'We might as well get on to business,' said Mother.

'Have you brought anything along?' asked Kurtz.

My mother opened her handbag and removed her pass and a piece of Ministry of Supply headed notepaper.

Kurtz was clearly expecting something more significant. Mother had the documents he wanted in her bag, but before she produced them, she glanced around the room and asked a nervous, instinctive question, as pointless as it was pertinent: 'Can anybody hear us here?'

'Oh my God, no!' he lied. 'There is only one flat next door, and the great advantage of this building is that it's quiet nowadays since the bombing. I like living in this place since the bombing. It is not at all *frequented*.' His English was near perfect, but not quite.

Mother produced a sheaf of papers which Kurtz began to sift through.

'What I've got is a lot of stuff about various factory sites and contracts with Northern Ireland for stuff. And also Southern Ireland, defence measures in Southern Ireland – Eire. I suppose you know about that – what is going on there.' Kurtz nodded. 'And shipments to Turkey, and something about some secret wireless transmitter ...'

'How were you able to get all these documents?' asked Kurtz. Mother explained that in her job as a typist, she was able to copy anything that looked as if it might be important.

Molly explained how easy this was. 'You see, Norah does work for more than one person,' she said. 'If ever she is doing anything, she can say she is working for somebody else, so you see they can't check up on her. They don't question it. It's too good to be true, somehow!' Indeed it was.

As Kurtz scanned the papers, he picked out significant details and read them out in a low voice. 'This is very interesting ... a meeting held on March 5th ... Yes, there you are, this is very interesting – not bad at all.' He ran his eye down the page and picked out the name of the head of Mother's department. 'You work for Colonel Webb?'

'Yes,' she answered. 'Goodness knows what he would think or what he would do if he saw me sitting here. It does amuse me so!'

'Well, I don't think he's under the settee,' said Kurtz.

In the kitchen, Sergeant Farnes wrote down the word 'laughter'.

Kurtz turned another page. 'I don't understand *this* exactly,' he said.

Mother explained that it was a list of power stations. And then she said something that I read with shame when I first saw it written down in Sergeant Farnes's transcript: 'It gives you an idea of what to get at.'

It gives you an idea of what to get at. Mother knew exactly what she was doing. She was suggesting targets for the enemy to bomb.

As Harald Kurtz scanned the rest of the papers, he read several words and phrases out loud. To Mother and Molly, it seemed that he was vocalising key words in the way people sometimes do when they skim through a document; in fact, he was reading them for the benefit of those listening in the kitchen. He was allowing them to decide how important these documents were. Whether it would be appropriate to pounce.

'. . . A shipment recently effected, fifteen lightning arresters, goods lost at sea . . . two thousand, six hundred pounds . . . This is very interesting,' remarked Kurtz.

At the sound of the turning lock, the two women's faces froze in shock. The kitchen door opened and Knight walked in, accompanied by Jones and Farnes.

'Who are you?' Harald Kurtz demanded, still keeping up the pretence that he wasn't in on the trick.

'We are police officers,' announced Jones. 'I suppose you realise you are under arrest?'

Mother never spoke to me about the moment of her arrest, and she says nothing of the events that led up to it and followed from it in her unpublished autobiography. But she wrote a thinly disguised account of her entrapment in her novel *No Complaints in Hell*. It is obvious that the details are remembered rather than invented: the authority in the voice of the character that is clearly based on Knight. The oddity of his dress – a grey pinstriped suit with carefully creased trousers, and the brown suede shoes that the character that is clearly Mother finds herself staring at. The drab young policewoman who leads the Mother character into the flat's small bathroom and orders her to strip. The feeling of powerlessness after the arrest. Being ordered to spit into the sink in case she had a suicide pill hidden in her mouth.

Mother wrote of the grey plain of concrete that stood bleakly before the flats as she was led outside after the arrest, and the big blue car that was waiting. She describes an atmosphere of almost lunatic friendliness in the vehicle, in which she felt invited to participate. But she didn't, sensing that behind her captors' excited relief lay the unexpressed outrage of a whole nation. She couldn't face provoking it now.

The early summer of 1941 was not a fortuitous time to be standing trial for treason. Feelings were running high. In London, the Blitz had reached a fiery crescendo on 10 May, in a raid in which 3,000 people were killed or injured. That night, the chamber of the House of Commons was destroyed by incendiaries, and the British Museum, St James's Palace, St Clement Dane's, the Royal Mint and the Tower of London were among many other historic buildings to be hit. The Old Bailey was left looking like an ornately iced cake from which a rough slice had been carved, leaving stone fragments scattered about like crumbs.

After ten months of near-continuous bombing, great swathes of the capital had been reduced to rubble. Jumbled piles of bricks and broken plaster marked the sites of tenements; terraces sported gaping holes like the stumps of badly broken teeth. The East End and the Docks had been pounded mercilessly and repeatedly. Whole streets and blocks of houses had been levelled or lay in dusty heaps. By May 1941, air raids had killed 43,000 British people and destroyed 1.4 million British homes. Such statistics weren't at everybody's fingertips, of course, but everybody knew the scale of the suffering; everybody recognised the Germans as a cruel and pitiless enemy that had to be resisted at all costs.

From her cell in the women's prison at Holloway, Mother must have heard the chilling howl of the sirens, the grinding roar of enemy aircraft and the crumps and bangs of exploding bombs. Perhaps she saw hope in the flames that fired the patch of sky she could glimpse through her high barred window. Maybe she imagined that the ferocity of the raids was a sign of a coming German invasion in which she would be not only liberated, but honoured for her fidelity to the Führer. I don't know exactly how she felt. But if she allowed herself such thoughts, they can have offered only brief comfort. She had been caught red-handed in an act of treachery, and beyond her prison walls, the battle-scarred nation that she had attempted to betray was waiting to exact vengeance.

There were two preliminary charges laid against Mother and Molly:

1. That on 15th March, 1941, with intent to help the enemy they were jointly concerned in doing or attempting to do an act which was designed or likely to give assistance to the naval, military or air operations of the enemy, to wit communicating information from the files of the Ministry of Supply. (Contrary to Section 1 of the Treachery Act, 1940.)

2. That on 15th March, 1941, with intent to assist the enemy they did an act which is likely to assist the enemy or to prejudice the public safety, the defence of the realm, or the efficient prosecution of the war, in that they were concerned jointly in communicating information from the files of the Ministry of Supply. (Contrary to Regulation 2A (1) of the Defence (General) Regulations, 1939.)

The first charge carried the mandatory death penalty; the second the possibility of imprisonment for life.

When Mother and Molly were told that the date for their trial was to be Monday 16 June, they must have started counting the days with increasing dread. Any thread of hope that they might have clung to was ominously severed on Friday the thirteenth, when their solicitor informed them of the outcome of a trial that had ended that day. In the very court where Mother and Molly were to appear, before the very judge who was to try them the following Monday, two Nazi spies, Karl Drucke (a German) and Werner Waelti (a Swiss), had faced charges under Section 1 of the Treachery Act. Arrested almost immediately after their arrival in a flying boat off the Scottish coast the previous September, they had achieved precisely nothing in their efforts to undermine the British war effort. They had been found guilty in a matter of minutes; Mr Justice Asquith had donned the black cap and pronounced the only sentence available to him. If the courts could show no mercy to two bungling foreigners, what pity could be expected for two treacherous subjects of the Crown?

As Mother and Molly Hiscox were driven from Holloway through a grey, war-weary London to the Old Bailey that Monday morning, they must have felt sick with fear. The bomb-breached building in which they were to answer for their lives was the very embodiment of the order they had sought to overturn. Above the half-wrecked west wing, the sword arm of Justice pointed accusingly at the skies from which the Luftwaffe had rained down so much high-explosive hate. Handcuffed, the two women were led through a wall of defensive sandbags into a place where the full significance of their actions was inescapable.

The evidence against them was overwhelming. It included not only the depositions of the agents who had been spying on them, the documents that Mother had given to Kurtz, and Sergeant Farnes's transcript of the conversation during which Mother had handed them over, but also the evidence found when both women's homes had been searched after their arrest. In Mother's flat, they found the letters of introduction to foreign Fascists that Vaughan-Henry had written for her in

June 1939. Her credentials as an internationally active anti-Semite were beyond doubt.

What they found among Molly Hiscox's stored possessions was even more damning. Along with a seven-by-eleven-and-a-half-inch Nazi flag, her membership cards for the British Union and the Link, and 'a number of photographs of Hitler and of Nazis in uniform', was the letter she had written to the Führer on the day that he had invaded Slovakia. It had been opened by the British Censor and returned undelivered.

The trial was held in camera. While they had been in Holloway, Molly had arranged the sale of the only thing of value that she owned – a café in Ewell High Street – to pay for their defence. This bought them the services of St John Hutchinson KC. Things did not look good, he told them. He advised that if they pleaded guilty to the capital offence, they would hang for sure; their only chance was to plead not guilty on that count, and hope that the prosecution's thirst for vengeance would be satisfied by their admission of guilt on the lesser charges that covered the same deeds. There was a slim chance that the Crown might withdraw the capital indictment.

The charges against Mother and Molly were read out. They had grown in the interval since their arrest: Molly now faced four; Mother five. The first three were common to both of them: that they had communicated confidential information to an unauthorised person; that they had been in possession of confidential documents; and that they had communicated information that might be of use to an enemy. Mother was additionally charged with undertaking an act likely to assist an enemy by taking copies of confidential files from the Ministry of Supply. All these were offences under the Defence (General) Regulations, 1939. The maximum penalty for each was life imprisonment. As each charge was read out, each prisoner admitted her guilt.

Then the last charge was put to them: that they had jointly 'conspired to do acts designed to assist the enemy, and with doing such an act, contrary to Section 1 of the Treachery Act 1940'.

The answer of each was 'not guilty', though both women knew that they had done exactly as the charge alleged.

The prosecuting counsel, G.B. McLure, rose to speak. He asked the judge for permission to withdraw the charges under the Treachery Act; Mr Justice Asquith took the request calmly and agreed. Mother and Molly's relief must have been palpable but short-lived – they were still facing the prospect of life imprisonment. Hutchinson rose and made his plea in mitigation. When he had finished, the court doors were thrown open to the public, and both defendants waited to hear how they were to be sentenced.

It seems that what Hutchinson had achieved was to present Mother and Molly as deluded and deranged rather than treacherous.

'Your crime is a political crime,' announced Mr Justice Asquith, 'and it is sometimes suggested that political crime ought to be treated with greater leniency than other crimes. I entirely dissent from that view. It seems that of all forms of crime, that affecting the State, at whose heart it is directed, can be least tolerated.' He did not confront Mother with her attempts to direct bombers and submarines towards tactically valuable targets. He did not pick up Molly's cruel remarks about the Bank Station bomb crater and throw them back at her. And though it was within his power to sentence them to life imprisonment, he gave each woman only five years. Their lives had been saved by the sale price of a Surrey teashop.

The following day, Guy Liddell met with Maxwell Knight. He summed up their conversation in his diary:

> Lunched with M. He told me all about the Briscoe case and showed me the documents. They are voluminous and cover a wide field. If the information had leaked it would certainly be a very serious matter. They relate to the location of factories, shortage of materials, establishment of submarine bases in N Ireland, etc.

But would the information have leaked? The Metropolitan Police Commissioner, Sir Norman Kendal, didn't think so. In a letter to the Home Office dated 27 March, he wrote: 'These people make one feel angry, but I do not think myself that they had much idea of how to get news to Germany.' He might have added that they would have had no idea at all if they hadn't been offered an opening by MI5 *agents provocateurs*. These days, we would call such an operation 'entrapment'. But I don't say that Mother didn't deserve to be trapped.

9

Total War

1942−45

You must learn to accept deprivations without ever collapsing. Regardless of whatever we create and do, we shall pass away, but in you, Germany will live on, and when nothing is left of us you will have to hold up the banner which some time ago we lifted out of nothingness.

Adolf Hitler, address to the Hitler Youth*

Life began to get difficult in 1942. Radio bulletins and cinema newsreels continued to report victories, but we didn't seem to be benefiting from them at home. Food was rationed, and other supplies were scarce. We were told to do our bit for the war effort by observing *Eintopf* – one-pot – Sundays, on which we would stretch what little food we had by making it all into a stew. This didn't seem too bad at first, but as time went by, the proportion of meat to vegetables got smaller and smaller.

*At the Nuremberg rally of 1934.

You couldn't get round it by going to a pub or a restaurant, because they had to observe *Eintopf* Sundays, too. Posters encouraging us to be frugal for the sake of the war effort began to appear everywhere. Stickers were placed over light switches telling us to save electricity for the Führer. Some necessities simply ran out. When I got a toothache, the dentist told me that if I wanted my teeth filled, I would have to bring him something with which to fill them; otherwise he would have to pull them out. Hildegard was horrified when I told her this, and she and Maria and Opa found some old silver jewellery and coins that they were prepared to sacrifice for me. I took it to the dentist, and I watched his assistant put it in a little crucible over a burner, melt it down, and skim off the dross, so that my teeth could be stopped with it. There were short-ages at school, too. When we ran out of paper, we wrote out our exercises on blank pages torn from the backs of textbooks and any other scraps we could find. When we couldn't get ink, we wrote in pencil.

We accepted that we had to put up with such things for the sake of the Führer, whose life was one constant sacrifice for the good of the *Volk*. I held him in far greater awe than anyone else at Möbelhaus Weyrich. I suppose I looked up to him as one might look up to a father. With Seppl and Willi away, the only other male in the household was Opa, and, much as I loved him, I didn't see him as a figure of authority. The Führer, though, was a father to all of us – confident, strong and wise, like Frederick the Great in the film *Der Grosse König*.* When

*'The Great King'.

I'd seen it in the Mainstrasse cinema that spring, it had moved me to tears.

But at the beginning of February 1943, we heard a special announcement on the wireless that threw the Führer's fatherly judgement into doubt:

> The Supreme Command of the Wehrmacht announces that the battle of Stalingrad has come to an end. True to its oath of allegiance, the Sixth Army under the exemplary leadership of Field Marshal Paulus has been annihilated by the over-whelming superiority of enemy numbers . . . They died so that Germany might live.

We could hardly believe it. All the reports we had heard in the last six months had been of victories. Nothing had prepared us for the news of such a huge defeat. There were a quarter of a million men in the Sixth Army. The idea that they had all been killed was unthinkable.* Three days of national mourning were declared, during which all radio broadcasts were to be replaced by solemn music.

Opa's face turned to stone, and Hildegard expressed outrage at whatever military bungling must have led to such a horrifying waste of life. Maria went off to find her copy of *Mein Kampf*, and referred us to a passage in which the Führer said no war should be fought on two fronts – and she reminded us that we had been fighting on three. Oma said

---

*In fact, they had not. Hitler could not bear to admit that many of the men he had ordered to fight to the death had surrendered. Around 91,000 were taken prisoner.

'that man' was a '*Dummkopf*'; I shuddered to hear anyone speak like that about our Führer. I didn't know what to think. I was a loyal member of the Hitler Youth. We had been told that it was our duty to report any dissenting voices or doubters, but I couldn't possibly denounce my own family – though I knew that some of the other boys had denounced theirs. Such talk upset me. It was treacherous. But I said nothing.

News of the defeat at Stalingrad was followed by another special announcement on the wireless. We were told that we were now fighting a 'total war' in which every man, woman and child had a part to play in the struggle for national survival. We heard extracts from a speech Dr Göbbels had made in the Berlin *Sportpalast*, which had been greeted with roars of approval by the audience. It sounded as if he was asking the whole nation whether it wanted to rededicate itself to the Führer, and the whole nation was shouting back 'yes'. What I didn't know was that everyone in the *Sportpalast* audience had been hand-picked, and the responses they yelled to Göbbels's questions had been rehearsed. What I did know was that in our family, at least, confidence in the Führer was fading fast. I know now that many others felt the same, but were too frightened to share their thoughts. But I wasn't one of them. In my mind, the Führer was beyond criticism. Three years in the HJ had taught me that. I loved my adopted country, and I had sworn an oath of loyalty to the man who personified it. I had no intention of deserting him now that things were getting tough. In any case, it wasn't as tough in Miltenberg as it was in the industrial regions or great cities, which had been heavily bombed by Allied aircraft. The centre of Lübeck had been destroyed on 28 March, and Cologne had suffered terribly in the thousand-bomber raid on 30 May 1942. Our part of the world was not an obvious target, but we could see the dark clouds of bombers moving across our skies to attack the places that were.

*

I am on the train from Amorbach to Miltenberg. It is early in the afternoon; the carriage is almost empty. The day is warm and all the windows are open. An old man in a soft cap is nodding off in the seat half opposite me. Spittle is dribbling from the corner of his mouth, which hangs half open, toothless. He doesn't notice. The swaying of the train has lulled him to sleep. At the far end of the carriage, two middle-aged women sit chatting quietly. One of them has a wicker basket on her lap. She reaches into it, takes out a chunk of black bread and a piece of cheese, breaks them in half and shares them with her neighbour. We are going downhill, and the train rocks slightly forwards and backwards as the carriages catch up with the engine and it picks up steam to pull away.

There is a sudden clattering and banging along the roof. The old man wakes with a start, and wipes his mouth with the back of his hand. One of the women screams. Her cry is drowned by the noise of an aeroplane engine that starts somewhere in front of us and roars off behind. I look out of the window and see a fighter with American markings. Is it a Mustang? I recognise it from the pictures we have been shown in the Hitler Youth. It is sleeker and more beautiful than those pictures suggest. The engine driver sounds his whistle and the train begins to pick up speed as the plane turns in a great arc to come back again. This is madness – there is no way we can outrun it, and there isn't a tunnel for miles. We take a bend so fast that I feel the carriage tilt, and I can see the luggage car, the coal tender and the engine curved out in front. Sparks as well as smoke are belching out of the funnel. Another roar, another rattle along the roof, and this time bullets rake through the boiler. The engine hisses, sighs and slows to a jerky halt. I see the driver jump out and run down the embankment. At the foot of it, he turns and beckons to the rest of us to do the same. The woman who screamed is now sobbing uncontrollably, and her companion is ushering her to the door. They struggle to descend the steps, and I decide to get out through the window. The old man has already done so – he is nimbler than he looks. We all help each other down the slope and huddle under a stand of oaks a few yards from the embankment. We wait for the plane's return, but it does not come. I catch my breath and realise that I am not afraid. I am exhilarated. War is exciting.

*

During the summer holidays, there was a lot of talk about whether or not it would be safe to carry on travelling to Amorbach in September, but in the event I didn't have to: I was transferred to the new secondary school that had recently been set up in Miltenberg, which was within walking distance.

I missed life at the Amorbach Gymnasium. There was something light-hearted about it. The atmosphere was relaxed and friendly. There were only fifty or so students, and every-body knew everybody else. Things at the Miltenberg *Oberschule* were quite different. The classes were bigger, and numbers were constantly increased by refugees. Many of these were Volksdeutsche, ethnic Germans who had settled in places as far away as the Black Sea, and who were now returning to the bosom of the fast-shrinking Reich. The teachers were all old and seemed to have been dragged unwillingly from retire-ment. There were never enough of them, and some classes contained as many as a hundred pupils. The education system was collapsing under the weight of a war that we were obviously losing, and there wasn't much learning going on.

The atmosphere in the town quickly changed. I no longer recognised most of the people I saw on the streets. The few Jews I had known of seemed to have drifted away – probably to live with relatives abroad, explained Oma, who added that one shouldn't ask about such matters, which were none of our business. More and more foreigners were seen – guest workers from the east, who were billeted in redundant buildings, and who worked on the land or in the factories. At first, they stuck out like sore thumbs with their strange clothes and accents, and their tired, lost-looking faces, but soon it was the native Miltenbergers that looked out of place, as the town filled up with strangers, including an increasing number of refugees. We began to see wounded soldiers back from the eastern front, tottering about on crutches or in invalid carriages like low prams. Many were missing arms and legs, which I assumed had been blown off in battle, but Hildegard told me that most had been amputated on account of frostbite. She said that some of the stories those men were telling were too terrible to repeat, so I could only guess at the sufferings they must have endured. We had been told at Hitler Youth meetings that when we saw a war veteran in the street, we should salute him, and I always did so with pride. I felt that it somehow linked me to his heroism, but of course, it didn't. The childishness of the idea was brought home to me when I saluted a man in uniform before noticing that both his sleeves were empty and pinned to his tunic. He looked at me blankly before walking on.

But in other ways I was growing up fast. I was only thirteen when Hildegard told me she was anxious about Seppl's infidelities when he was away from home. She asked me to keep her worry a secret, but everybody knew what Seppl was like – what he got up to when his wife wasn't around was common knowledge. 'I know he can't help himself,' Hildegard explained. 'But it hurts.' She told me that she was going to make a pilgrimage to Engelberg to pray for his safe return and the survival of their marriage. She asked me if I would accompany her, and of course I said yes. The route to the church at Engelberg went through the Spessart forest north of the river. I didn't like the idea of her walking through all those forbidding oak trees with so many strangers about. I told her so. I was happy to look after her. As we ascended the hill to the church, I knelt beside her at each of the shrines that represented the Stations of the Cross, the scenes of Christ's sufferings and crucifixion. She was so lost in still and silent prayer that she seemed to become part of each tableau, a living witness to all that scourging, mocking and nailing. A few short years ago, I would have been moved by the thought of the sufferings endured for us all by the Saviour. Now, though, I found myself wondering why a man who claimed to be an all-powerful God would put up with it. It seemed as ungodly as it was unmanly. But I did not share these thoughts with Hildegard. I felt it would have been cruel to challenge her honestly held beliefs.

I was also called upon to play the man in other ways. Rations were so meagre that we could barely survive on them. The bread we got tasted of sawdust, and it wasn't made better by spreading it with *Kunsthonig*, a kind of artificial honey that was cloyingly sweet. Our coffee, too, was *ersatz* – artificial. It was made of roasted barley, which is just what it tasted like. We had meat, but it came in the form of sausages. What went into them was anybody's guess, but, whatever it was, it had been reduced to something like slime. The only way of supplementing a diet like this was by bartering for extras. We didn't dare do that in town, under the noses of the authorities, and if any of the adults went off carrying goods and came back carrying food, they might be caught. But a child wandering the countryside would be assumed to be at play. That, at least, is what I hoped – but it was a risky business, and I didn't dare to think what might happen to me if I was spotted by the *Volkssturm** or forest rangers. I avoided the danger by getting up at dawn, when I set off with a rucksack packed with small goods from the shop and sneaked out of town to barter for bacon and butter at local farms. I wore dark clothes and kept to the shadows. I started out barefoot, carrying my boots so

*Home guard.

that they wouldn't clatter on the cobbles. I stopped to put them on after I had slipped through the narrow opening in the tower in the town wall. Then I would scramble through the dark cut in the mountain called the *Schnatterloch* – the 'chattering hole'. It was called that because of the noise the water made when it ran down it in the spring and the winter – but in summer it was soundless and forbidding. I picked my way through nettles and brambles, under the old stone road bridge and into the forest of tall beeches above. Then I would look back to make sure I hadn't been followed, and watch the washed-out watercolour of the river valley resolve itself into an oil painting, glowing under the rising sun. Sometimes, the picture was so beautiful that it held me there for I don't know how long, for time seemed to stop while I looked at it. I loved what I saw. It was mine, and I was part of it.

My route took me across the *Felsenmeer*, a sea of huge red sandstone rocks set among trickling streams. After that came a dense plantation of firs, whose branches knitted together so tightly that little light reached the ground beneath. I always ran for this part of the journey. There was something lifeless about the dark. I didn't like it. I reached the meadows above with a sense of relief. I began to see signs of human habitation – fences, barns, farmhouses and the wayside shrine that marked the edge of the village of Monbrunn. Frau Mönch's house was only a few hundred yards away now. I always called on her, and she was always pleased to see me. Even if she didn't want anything I had brought from the shop, she would offer me something to eat – and it would be real food, farm food, food that I could taste.

I didn't walk straight up to the house. I would bend down as if to tie up a bootlace, and look back to make sure I wasn't being followed or watched. Only then would I stride up and knock on the door, which would be opened by a smiling Frau Mönch. How different her cheerful, round face was from the pale, grey features of those who lived in the town far below! She always greeted me with two questions: '*Was hast du gebracht?*' – 'What have you brought?' – and, after I had shown her the contents of my bag, '*Hast du Hunger?*' – 'Are you hungry?' – to which there was invariably the same answer. She would pick up a loaf of home-made bread and clasp it to her side to cut off a thick slice for me. Out would come the butter – white as snow, and glistening with coldness from the larder. A great pot of strawberry jam would appear, and she would make me a sandwich that more than repaid the efforts of my journey. Sometimes, there would even be a glass of buttermilk. Then I would pack my rucksack with rye bread, fat bacon, eggs, butter and sometimes a jar of real honey, and it would be time to go. '*Mach's gut, Paul!*' ('All the best!'), she would say. And, without fail: '*Sei vorsichtig!*' ('Be careful!'). I always was.

I was a different person when I was high above Miltenberg in the Odenwald. When I walked up to Monbrunn I left the war behind. I forgot about the Führer and the Hitler Youth and the rallies and the Jews and the Communists. All that was in a separate compartment of life. When I slipped back into Miltenberg with my contraband, I re-entered that compartment without a thought.

In the summer of 1944 I turned 14 and moved up from the Jungvolk to the main section of the Hitler Youth. The weekly meetings were much more serious than those I had been attending as a *Pimpf*. Now we had a stricter marching drill, followed by lectures on the evils of Bolsheviks and Jews, and the glorious national vision of the Führer. We were taught to recognise anti-German behaviour and told that it was our duty to report it. Anti-German behaviour included buying or selling on the black market, but I simply shut out the thought that it was something I did myself. Attendance was an absolute obligation, and to be absent from an *Appel* – a parade – was tantamount to desertion. On one occasion, Maria wouldn't let me go because I hadn't finished my homework. It didn't happen again, because our Gruppenführer came to the shop the very next day to point out that if I missed another meeting, there would be trouble. He then started calling meetings on Sunday mornings, deliberately timed to clash with mass. They were designed to be more attractive than mass, too. While the women and old men were at their prayers, our rising generation was enjoying adventure training in camp-craft and skiing in the forest, or rowing and swimming down at the river. When our parish priest complained, he got the same answer as our parents: nothing was to stand in the way of the *Appel*. Oma and Hildegard thought this outrageous, but I didn't complain. I was fast losing interest in religion. It had begun to seem unmanly and weak.

I threw myself into HJ life with enthusiasm. Discipline was tough, but there was a sense of camaraderie and common purpose. I let the political lecturing go over my head – I suspect we all did – but in every practical sense, I joined in. The reward was a warm sense of belonging. We were building a new Germany, and I was part of it. My unit was a branch of the HJ's naval section. We wore a naval uniform: a top with a striped collar, bell-bottomed trousers, and a sailor's cap with two blue ribbons hanging from the back and *Marine Hitler Jugend* printed on a band on the front. My brass belt buckle had an anchor on it, and I would polish it until it gleamed. We were miles from the sea, of course, but we had the River Main on our doorstep. We were taught how to row, how to send signals by Morse code and semaphore, and how to knot and splice ropes.

Shortly after I joined, one of our meetings was addressed by a Party official who told us that we were to be going off on a very un-naval adventure. We and all the other units* in our *Gau* were to help with the hop harvest. The BDM girls would be going, too. At first I thought he was asking for volunteers, but it was soon clear that we were all going whether we wanted to or not. We stood to attention as he read us our marching orders from a piece of paper. Everything had been planned down to the last detail.

We were being sent to Au, a small town north of Munich. We would stay there for a fortnight. We were to travel in uniform, taking a second set of clothes in which to work. We would work eight hours a day, Saturdays included. The BDM girls would join us in the fields when they were not cooking or washing. On Sundays we would be free to attend meetings, and then rest. Tools, baskets and stools would be provided. Bed spaces and sleeping areas were to be inspected daily. We

*A Hitler Youth unit was called a *Fähnlein*, which literally means 'little flag'.

would be paid generously and allowed to keep a small amount of our pay as pocket money; we would donate the rest to the Red Cross who looked after our brave soldiers, and to *Winterhilfe** to buy blankets and warm clothes for the needy. The band was to take its instruments. First-aid kits would be provided. We would be given a beer ration of a litre a day.

None of us moved or spoke, but we could all sense each other's excitement. The whole thing sounded like a marvellous adventure: a fortnight away from home with all those girls and beer, too – it had to be too good to be true! On the appointed day, we all marched behind our band and flags to the station. Oma and Hildegard were among the crowd of parents that waved us off. We broke into song as the train pulled out. We felt like heroes and holidaymakers both at once. The journey took all day, because we took a cross-country route, collecting carriages of other youngsters at various stations. When we finally got to Au, our engine whistle seemed to sound a note of joy mixed with relief.

We had lots of fun that fortnight, but it wasn't quite the treat we had expected. The beer turned out to be *Nährbier* with very little alcohol in it, and I worked so hard that I was too tired even to think about sex. If any of the other boys and girls managed to get up to anything like that, I didn't notice. The work was tough, but it was happy and purposeful. All two hundred of us would sit down beside the rows of hop wires strung out between posts, and our leaders would untie the

*Winter Aid – a fund originally started by the Nazi Party to help the unemployed survive the winter.

wires so that the vines would fall to the ground. Our job was to strip off the flowers and put them in baskets. When the baskets were full, we had to tip them into sacks that were taken by cart to the drying barns. We sang and told stories to each other as we worked.

One day, we all saw something extraordinary and inexplicable. A boy looked up from his hop-picking and noticed three grey aeroplanes in the sky. They were moving fast and low, but they weren't making any sound. He pointed up at them, and the whole field of us lifted our heads to stare. Only as they disappeared over the horizon did we hear the roar of their engines. The sound followed them across the sky and then was gone. Nobody could understand how the planes and the noise of them had become separated. We thought it must be the secret weapon that we had heard was going to win the war for us. It was the only time I heard the word 'war' mentioned during the entire fortnight.

After suppers cooked by the BDM in an army field kitchen, we sat around the campfire and sang together before settling down to sleep. Our beds were straw mattresses laid out in rows in a long bunkhouse. I was so tired that I fell asleep almost immediately, despite all the snoring and the scuttling of rats. Then, too soon, we would be startled into wakefulness by a reveille call on a bugle. This was the low point of the day, but we quickly got over it. On the last morning, the bugler found that his instrument had been plugged with bread and filled with ink. He was furious, but the rest of us laughed heartily at his misfortune. I don't remember laughing like that until long after the war.

It is hot. A suffocating quilt of humid air is sitting over Miltenberg, and a gang of us have gone down to the river to cool off. We have splashed about and frolicked, but not for long; it is too hot. Now, I am just bobbing and floating, watching the blurred reflection of the bridge tremble on the water. A couple of the other boys have swum back and are lazily wading towards the clothes they have left at the river's edge. They are chatting, but I can't hear what they are saying. I am too far out. Their voices seem to carry towards me and then fall away. I put back my head, close my eyes, give a little scissor kick, and waggle my hands just enough to keep afloat on my back.

Suddenly, a great roar rolls down and over me, and I feel the air judder and shake. I look up and see the tail of a bomber racing up the valley. Then another roar, this one so loud that I flinch, and I see the underbelly of a second American bomber fill the sky above me. It is gone in a moment, but it is so low that I can see the face of the man in the bubble of glass that houses the rear machine gun. He is a Negro – the first real live black man I have ever seen. As he flashes past, the sun glints on the gold watch on his wrist. As I stare, he starts firing. At first, I am not afraid – I am surprised. What is he shooting at? There aren't any soldiers about and he surely can't be aiming at us. But he is. I watch in disbelief as a burst of fire sends up a line of splashes that run across the water. The last one stops just short of me, but by then, the plane has started turning for a second run. I thrash my way to the bank in a blind panic. There is a haycart a few yards from the edge, and I throw myself under it. There are several other boys there already – boys I don't recognise, who make no effort to move to make room for me. I huddle by the edge and hug the ground. My heart is pounding so hard that it hurts, and I can scarcely catch my breath. When I tilt my head just far enough to see what is happening, I see the first plane bank away without firing, while the other one begins another run along the valley.

Through the spokes of the cartwheel, I watch bullets rip up the earth towards a group of potato pickers running for cover on the other side of the river. They are poorly dressed, and look like guest workers or refugees. Most of them manage to dive into a ditch for safety, but one woman is carrying a small child and has fallen behind. I lie there, willing her to run faster and get to safety, but she stumbles, and before she can recover her stride, a bullet flings the baby from her arms. The plane veers away, leaving a strange silence hanging in the air. The scene seems to freeze, and I find myself holding my breath. Then the woman slowly raises her hands to her head and begins a long, low moan that rises to a scream. As she rushes forward to pick up the body, I look away. I am overwhelmed – not by horror or pity, but by relief. I have survived.

I have seen the enemy who has to be resisted at all costs. He is every bit as savage as I have been taught. His face makes me think of the natives that the English had armed in *Ohm Krüger*. The idea that our troops would ever fire on unarmed women and children is unthinkable, but I have seen the enemy doing it in that film, and now I have just seen them doing it in real life.

Talk at home became increasingly defeatist. In early June we had been told that an Allied assault upon the Atlantic Wall had been repulsed, but we continued to hear news of fighting in France. We could see for ourselves that we had lost control of the skies above Germany: they were now filled with wave after wave of enemy bombers. We hardly ever saw any of our own planes attacking them; Maria told me that they couldn't because the Luftwaffe had run out of fuel. There certainly wasn't any fuel to be had for cars owned by civilians. Carts drawn by horses or bullocks appeared in the streets. We began to hear stories from wounded soldiers that did not tally with those that were told on the wireless. One announcement we did believe was one that nobody would have dared to make up. On 20 July, an attempt was made to assassinate the Führer. To me, this was nothing short of sacrilege, but the rest of the family did not seem to share my outrage. When I voiced my feelings, they fell silent and exchanged looks.

Everybody seemed to be concerned with surviving rather than winning the war. The only ones to keep faith with the Führer were the Hitler Youth. We were certain that he wouldn't fail us, and when we heard that V-1 and V-2 rockets were heading across the sky to England, we felt confident that it was only a matter of time before we would be celebrating the victory that he had promised. When we paraded, we listened to the exhortations of our leaders eagerly. They told us what we wanted to hear. Our country had its back to the wall, and it was up to us to do all we could to defend it. With the men away fighting at the front, it had fallen to us to keep the flag flying high at home.

I didn't just want to fight for the Fatherland, I wanted to die for it. I began to imagine meeting all sorts of heroic ends at the hands of its enemies. I wondered what it would feel like to be shot, perhaps while defending my family against Russian savages at the very door of Möbelhaus Weyrich. I would suffer, but that suffering would surely be glorious. I wanted the war to reach Miltenberg so that I could play a real part in it. I wanted to give myself and to give myself utterly, and there is no nobler act of giving than to suffer a selfless death.

I was too young to fight, but at least I could play a part in the nation's defences. At the end of 1944 I joined the team of old men and boys and girls that made up Miltenberg's *Feuerwehr*, the auxiliary fire service. I was issued with a uniform that was more practical than dashing – a heavy khaki tunic and trousers, and a black steel helmet with a leather flap to cover the back of the neck. I was taught how to use gas masks and to couple hoses, and how to treat broken limbs and burns. I was taught how to recognise and tackle incendiaries and to steer clear of bombs that contained high explosives. I was shown how to use and service our own fire engine, a hand-operated pump on a cart that we pulled or pushed. It was hung with buckets, which were to be filled using stirrup pumps to put out small fires our hoses could not reach. At first there weren't any fires of any size, because the Allies weren't dropping bombs, they were dropping propaganda leaflets. It was our job to gather these in before they could be read. We were also sent to pick up the strips of foil that enemy planes threw out to confuse our radar equipment. More and more of it was falling as the number of Allied aircraft in the skies increased.

Then the bombs came. The first fell without warning: a land mine that was probably dropped miles away and drifted in on its parachute until it got to the far side of Miltenberg, where it blew up several houses. It fell at night, and the sound of the explosion woke us all up. We thought it was a raid, so we all rushed down to the cellar. Oma and Opa had made it as comfortable as possible, and, as air-raid shelters go, it was pretty luxurious. Opa had found an offcut of carpet to cover the floor, and there were armchairs, a couple of beds and several candlesticks. But there was also a huge earthenware crock of fermenting sauerkraut in the corner, and the smell of it hung unhealthily in the air. We spent more and more time down there as the war drew to its bleak conclusion above. We passed the time playing endless games of cards for matchsticks. We were hungry and cold as well as bored. In the candlelit damp, my hopes of a glorious death gloomily dribbled away.

*

It isn't a dream, but it feels like one. A huge spar of wood is spinning slowly towards me through the air. I try to put up my arm to defend myself, but it won't move fast enough – it feels as if I am dragging the arm through water. The inside of my head turns into a kaleidoscope. I marvel at the sparking patterns of light. Only then do I hear the sound, and then everything speeds up. A great, roaring boom rises up and rushes towards me from the other side of the woodyard where I have been standing in a queue with my handcart, waiting to collect our ration of firewood for the week. Time seems to be moving backwards. I only hear the yard foreman shout 'Take cover!' after the bomb has exploded and I have been knocked onto my back. At first I feel nothing, but when I try to get up, my legs won't move and a hammering begins inside my head. Dust is settling slowly through the air around and above me, and I can hear the sound of bells and running water. For a moment, I imagine myself dozing by a rushing stream high in the mountains, with cattle clanking lazily in the distance. I put up my hand to wipe my face, but I freeze. My fingers are covered in blood, and one of them is split open to the bone.

*

The man pushing me along in my own handcart told me he had found me wandering dazed in the street. He was taking me to the hospital, and he was sure that I would be all right. I passed out, and when I came to I was sitting on a bench with dozens of other injured men, women and children. Somebody shouted 'Der Nächste!' ('Next!') and I felt myself being half ushered, half carried into a room where a masked surgeon stood behind an operating table. A nun in a bloodstained pinafore poured some liquid on a piece of cotton wool, held it to my face and told me to count out loud to ten. I don't think I got further than three or four before I fell unconscious. The next thing I knew I was standing in the street. I started to walk home, but it was difficult, because my left leg had been strapped up at the knee, and I couldn't bend it. My left hand was thickly bandaged, and a small red patch at the end of it was growing bigger as I looked at it. When I got home, Hildegard threw her arms around me and wept. She had gone to the woodyard to look for me, and when she had seen the huge crater near where she knew I would have been standing, she had assumed I had been blown to bits.

The bandaging on my hand was completely blood-soaked now. Hildegard gently unwrapped it and it was obvious that my stitches had burst. She bound it up again carefully and the bleeding stopped, but when she changed the dressing a couple of days later, the wound had become infected and she took me back to the hospital, where she was given a silver nitrate pencil with which to clean the wound. It made the skin on my hand bubble up and burn, and the pain of it was awful. The first time she used it, I passed out. Later, I knew what was coming and learned to put up with it. The injury put an end to my career in the Hitler Youth fire service. I never did get to put out a real fire. But my war wound did win me a bronze medal, which Gruppenführer Faust pinned to my chest at an HJ *Appel* some weeks later. He gave a little speech that made it sound as if I had done something heroic, pointing out that if the arm had been amputated, I would have won a silver medal. Hildegard told me later that I had been much nearer to winning one than I had known. The raid in which I was injured ended my German education. The primary target had been the power station, which was next door to the school. Both had been levelled by direct hits.

Time dragged. We were weak with hunger. Maria said that people had started eating dogs and cats; there certainly weren't any to be seen about the streets. Christmas 1944 came and went. Oma and Hildegard went to mass, but I didn't. There was no tree, and there were no presents, and if there was snow, I don't remember it. Defeat was in the air, from which more and more bombs were now falling. Streams of refugees heading for central Germany were making their way through streets littered with leaflets and anti-radar strips. Some were pushing perambulators piled with pots and pans and blankets; others walked beside farm carts stacked with possessions and furnishings and drawn by emaciated cattle and horses. They were fleeing the Americans and British in the west, and the Russians in the east. It was only a matter of time before both enemy advances met.

The first sign that the ground war had reached us was the destruction of the bridge. It took the whole town by surprise, because there had been no air-raid warning, and there were no planes to be seen in the sky. The first we knew of it was a series of explosions that came from the direction of the river. I ran back into the shop and rushed down to the cellar. The rest of the family were there already. We waited a while, but there were no more bangs, and no siren. Oma said that there was something different about the sound of the explosions. We agreed. There was something snappier about them, and the intervals between them had been regular. After a while it was obvious that there hadn't been an air raid, and we climbed the stone steps to daylight and went out onto the Marktplatz. Other people were surfacing and gathering to talk. Someone said that the bridge had been hit, and we all made our way down to the river to see what had happened.

MY FRIEND THE ENEMY

What we saw when we turned the corner made us stop and stare in horror. The old bridge, which had seemed as permanent as the landscape, had been destroyed. The gate tower on our side of the river was standing guard over a handful of pillars with nothing in between. On some of them, bits of wreckage were hanging. When we got closer, we saw that one now held up the remains of a cart. Another had become a perch for an undamaged bicycle. On the one right out in the middle stood a howling dog. Below us, people were fishing a woman's body out of the water. There was nothing we could do, so we went back to the shop in silence. Opa fell behind and turned up later, smelling of drink. I don't know where he would have got any, but he must have managed it somehow. When he came into the sitting room, he was angry and keen to show it. He told us that he had found out that the bridge had been blown up by our own troops. An SS detachment had done it without warning the people crossing it. It had been pointless: the Americans wouldn't be here for days or weeks yet, and they had floating bridges that could cross the river 'just like that', he said, snapping his fingers. 'So much for your wonderful Führer!' he said to nobody in particular. Then he offered the room a *Hitlergruss* and spat.

Easter fell on 1 April 1945, but nobody in Miltenberg was celebrating or playing practical jokes. The self-sacrifice of Lent was not over – it was only just beginning. Hildegard had got a telegram informing her that Seppl was missing in action, and she fell into a mood that alternated between mourning and hope. Holy Week had been marked not by festive preparations, but by salvos of artillery fire getting closer and closer.

On Maundy Thursday, a silence had gathered over the town, though we could hear the rumble of tanks in the distance. In the afternoon, a buzzing speck in the sky became a light aircraft, which scattered pieces of paper that drifted the ground like hesitant snow. People picked them up, even though it was forbidden. Soon, we would have a new master to answer to, and we wanted to know what was expected of us. The message on the first leaflet was unambiguous. We were told that if we didn't surrender, the town would be taken by force. On Good Friday, a single plane dropped a second message. It was an open letter addressed to the Bürgermeister – our mayor. He was told to present himself at the west of the town, carrying a white flag.

Oma said the Bürgermeister was bound to obey, and we should all get down in the cellar and wait to see what happened. After a while, I grew impatient and ran up the cellar steps. I stood in the doorway, ignoring Hildegard's calls for me to come back down to safety. I saw the Bürgermeister cross the square, holding up a piece of white cloth as tall as he was. Maria called up to ask me what was happening, but I ignored her. The Marktplatz was empty and the whole town was still. When the Bürgermeister reappeared, I saw him roll up his improvised flag and tuck it inside his jacket. I ran down to tell the others what I had seen. Halfway down the steps, I heard a burst of machine-gun fire, and I turned round to see where it had come from. I peered around the door, and there were more shots that seemed to be coming from the castle. Oma shouted up to ask what was happening. Hildegard yelled at me to come down. When the shelling started, I did as I was told. A dozen or so rounds whistled overhead and crumped into the hillside above us. We waited for more, but they didn't come, and everything was once again silent. Nobody spoke. Hildegard got out her rosary, and she and Oma quietly mumbled the prayers together. We didn't hear the plane that dropped a second message from the sky. It had been an ultimatum, and the Bürgermeister had accepted it. What we did hear was the sudden revving of scores of tanks down by the river, then the sound of them squealing, jangling and clattering up the hill.

*

He is as black as Knecht Ruprecht, and far more frightening. He lurches around the corner waving a machine gun as if it is a swagger stick. He is dressed from head to foot in camouflage, and his helmet is pushed back on his head. Several looted cameras swing from his neck, and he is chewing. I haven't come across chewing gum before – I imagine he is grinding his teeth like a beast. I want to turn and run, but I am frightened that if I move suddenly, he might shoot me. I stand still and try to look unthreatening. He is only ten yards away when he notices me. He stops, raises his gun, and then lets it fall, as if he just can't be bothered to fire it. 'Schnapps,' he calls out, making signs of drinking from a bottle, 'Schnapps!' I can't help him. I don't have any. There isn't any. I don't know what to say to him, but before I can think of something, he is gone, stumbling on the cobblestones and muttering what I guess must be a curse.

*

From the corner of the shop window I watched the troops pull into the Marktplatz. Several troop carriers and a tank rolled to a halt by the fountain, where the sports car had been parked for *Spiel im Sommerwind* seven years earlier. A very different scene was being acted out now. The soldiers who jumped out of the vehicles fanned out and entered every building, kicking in or shooting open any doors that were locked. Anyone they found was sent to stand outside and wait. Before they got to the shop, I called down to the rest of the family and told them to come upstairs quickly so that we could be seen to co-operate. Opa unlocked the front door so that it wouldn't be beaten down, but the two Americans who turned up a moment later kicked it in without trying the handle. They pointed their machine guns at us and motioned for us to get out. We stumbled out with our hands in the air and joined the line of our neighbours standing silently in the Marktplatz. None of them had their hands up, so we dropped ours, but a soldier came along immediately and grabbed my wrist and held it up. He was looking to see if I was wearing a watch. I wasn't. Opa realised what was happening and discreetly unfastened the pocket watch from his waistcoat and slipped it into the back pocket of his trousers.

We weren't kept standing there for long before we were dismissed. Everybody went back indoors to see what damage had been done and what had been looted. We were surprised to find the place exactly as we had left it, but then I don't suppose our occupiers had much immediate use for rolls of lino or pieces of furniture, and the few scraps of food in our larder had not been touched. We stayed indoors for the rest of the day, not daring to go out, in case it was against whatever regulations had now been imposed on us. We were frightened of doing anything that might get us arrested or shot. We were used to regarding laws and regulations as absolute; the penalties for breaking our own laws had been mercilessly applied. We soon found out what the new rules were. Large posters appeared all over the town, and people gathered anxiously to read them. The rule that affected us most immediately was the curfew: we weren't allowed on the streets after dark.

Miltenberg was suddenly full of uniforms, and most of the soldiers wearing them were black. We had been conquered by men whom we had been taught to consider our inferiors. We could see from the way that their white officers spoke to them that they thought them inferior, too. What further confused matters was that Maria said she was sure that several of those officers were Jews. As if that were not enough of a sign that our world had been turned upside down, the occupying Americans established their headquarters in the boarded-up Miltenberg synagogue.

*

In early May, we had a family conference. Oma said that now the war was over we were going to have to rebuild the business and fit in with the occupying regime. She had thought of a way to get on the right side of the Americans: she would tell them that the family had sheltered an English boy for the whole of the war. I had no objection – after all, it was true, and I was grateful to them for it. If Hildegard and Seppl hadn't adopted me, I would certainly have been interned in some sort of camp. So Hildegard looked out my birth certificate and I took it down to the American HQ.

The last time I had been in that building was on 10 November 1938. I wish I could say that my memories of that night's events made returning uncomfortable, but the truth is that I was not then troubled by guilt. My feelings were not of remorse, but of surprise. When I was shown to a desk at the back of the room to see the duty officer, standing behind him was Heinz Faust, my ex-HJ Gruppenführer. Before I could speak, he said something about me in English to the American and then addressed me in German as if I were a stranger. What he said was that whatever I did, I wasn't to mention anything about his role in the HJ, but the American clearly didn't understand what he was saying – he nodded in approval as he spoke. Then the officer addressed me directly in English and was surprised when I looked at him blankly, unable to understand. But whatever Faust said to him next clearly persuaded him that I really was the person named on my birth certificate, because he dictated a letter for Faust to type, signed it and stamped it and told me to take it to the *Landratsamt* – the District Council Office.

There, I presented the letter to a clerk who was astonished to be given instructions to issue a passport. Nobody from Miltenberg had needed one for years, and he wasn't even sure where the blank books were kept. I watched him rummage through all his filing cabinets and cupboards, and he eventually found one of the sort he needed: a *Fremdenpass* – a passport for issue to foreigners. He carefully opened it and folded it back so that it lay flat on the desk in front of him. I read it upside down as he wrote my name on the front page. Immediately underneath was printed '*Der Passinhaber besitzt nicht die Deutsche Reichsangehörigkeit*' – 'The bearer does not have German nationality'. I asked him whether he was sure that this was the right sort of passport to give me, and he insisted that it was – the letter from the American colonel was perfectly clear. It didn't seem right to me, but if that was what my family wanted, I didn't mind. Everybody knew I was German really; but if it suited my family to pretend to the occupiers that I wasn't, that was fine by me.

The clerk turned the page and filled in '*England*' for my nationality. It was a double mistake, but I let it pass. Beside 'Distinguishing Marks' he wrote '*Halsnarbe und Narben an der linken Hand*' – scar on the neck and scars on the left hand. (My war wounds left marks that I carry to this day.) He glued in my photograph and secured it with two metal rivets, and reached for a large, wooden-handled rubber stamp. He inked it and raised his arm, but stopped before the stamp hit the paper. He put it back on the inkpad and sighed. Then he reached into his pocket, brought out a penknife, and cut the swastika out of the middle of the wreath below the eagle. My personal denazification had begun.

*

Life in occupied Miltenberg was difficult. I didn't dare slip up the mountain to barter for extra food; there were too many patrols about. We were able to barter with the Americans; not for necessities like bread, eggs or butter, but for treats that brought a little colour into our drab, defeated lives. They had chocolate, chewing gum, Coca-Cola and cigarettes. We had Nazi mementoes that we were only too pleased to part with. Hildegard had cut the insignia from my HJ uniforms, and Opa had buried them in a tin box in the garden, along with my *Leistungsbuch* and anything else that linked me with my Nazi past. When we realised that some of these things were valued by the Americans, Opa dug up the box and took out my badges, belt buckles and buttons. It was depressing rather than painful to part with them. They seemed totally meaningless now that everything they represented had been destroyed. But I did feel a lump in my throat when Opa took out my *Fahrtenmesser*. I slipped it out of its sheath and admired its blade one last time before he took it away to trade for a Hershey bar and a packet of Lucky Strikes.

Willi came back to Miltenberg at the end of June, and he and Maria moved back into their apartment on the other side of town. But by mid-July there was still no news of Seppl. Hildegard was clinging to the hope that he would somehow turn up. Lots of others had; the war seemed to have ended in complete confusion, and some people had appeared after they had been reported dead. Oma wasn't so sure. Hildegard spoke of how things would be *when* Seppl came back; the word that Oma used was '*if*'. She also said we would have to think about what to do if he didn't. The business would need a man to run it, and she wanted that man to be a member of the family. If it couldn't be Seppl, she wanted that man to be me. She didn't ask me whether I would want to do it when I was old enough; she assumed that I would, and she was right.

In July a black Mercedes staff car drew up outside Möbelhaus
Weyrich. A few months earlier, it would have been flying a
swastika; now, the little flag that fluttered on its bonnet was
British. The arrival caused quite a stir, because we were in the
American zone, and the people in the car were the first British
soldiers we had seen. One of them climbed out and came into
the shop. Oma was behind the counter and he addressed her
in English, which she couldn't understand, but the man was
repeating my name and had clearly come to the right place.
Maria hurried down to the synagogue to get someone to
translate. She came back with the well-fed and denazified
Heinz Faust, who explained that the captain had been ordered
to check if I was still alive and, if I was, to tell me that arrange-
ments would be made to take me home. I couldn't think what
he could mean. 'Home to England,' he replied. 'Home to your
mother.'

I told him that I didn't want to go, but he said that his
orders were to simply tell me this news; what happened next
had nothing to do with him. He had no idea how long it
would be before transport would be organised. It could be
days, weeks or months. Somebody would inform me nearer
the time.

The idea was absurd. I couldn't even remember what
Mother looked like. I hadn't thought of her for years. I
thought of Hildegard as my mother, and with Seppl gone, it
was my duty to look after her. I couldn't leave Opa with no
one to talk to, and I owed it to Oma to help her run the family

business – *our* family business. Why would I want to abandon them to live with someone that I hadn't seen since the summer of 1939, and who hadn't even written to me for the last four years ? What would I say to her? Whatever it might be, it couldn't be in her native language. I had forgotten all but a half-dozen words of English. No. I wouldn't go. I loved my Fatherland, my foster family and my home.

Hildegard told me not to worry. Seppl was bound to turn up soon, and he would know what to do. In any case, the soldier who had tracked me down had admitted that he had no idea how long it would take to organise getting me sent back; there must be more important things for the occupying troops to worry about than deporting an uncooperative fifteen-year-old boy. The war had left displaced persons stranded all over Europe. There were hundreds of thousands of people who wanted to get back to their real homes, and they would surely be attended to first. In all the confusion, my case would very likely be filed away and forgotten.

*

They came for me in early October. This time, the officer spoke enough German to make his simple message clearly understood: I had half an hour to pack and then I was to be taken to the British consulate in Frankfurt. I should say my goodbyes now because I wouldn't be coming back. If I had known beforehand that they were coming, I would have run away. I could even have run away then, but the suddenness of it all shocked us into obedience. Where was Hildegard? Opa said that she had gone off to queue for our meat ration, and he hurried out to find her and bring her back. Oma, meanwhile, was rushing about, pulling open drawers and flinging their contents into the imitation-leather suitcase that Mother had bought me six years ago for five marks. Hildegard ran through the front door in tears and flung her arms around me. The officer looked away in embarrassed silence. Everybody was rushing about, frantically fetching a coat, a pair of boots, some shirts, my stamp collection, some socks, a piece of bread, an apple, my vaccination certificates. And a hat – yes, I had to have a hat, Hildegard said; no, my old HJ cap wasn't suitable; here, take Opa's (a traditional Tyrolean hat with a tuft in it like a shaving brush); everybody in England wears a hat. Where is his passport? Here, take this money, you might need it . . .

I stood silently in the middle of all this activity, the still centre in the spinning world of a terrible dream. I wanted to weep, but the tears wouldn't come. I wanted to say that this was all ridiculous, it was so absurd that it couldn't really be happening, but I couldn't get the words out of my mouth. I felt as if I had no more control of my body than I had of events. The soldier looked at his watch and nodded through the window to his driver, and I watched him come in, pick up my bag and put it in the boot. Then I was standing by the car door, and he was holding it open for me. A crowd of neighbours and strangers had gathered to watch. What's he done? Has he been arrested? Their voices seemed strangely muted, as if heard through water. *Auf wiedersehen, Paulchen!* Write – promise you will write! Come back to us! Promise you will come back! Hildegard flung her arms around me; Maria came running into the Marktplatz just in time to snatch me and give me a hug. Oma did the same, and Opa stepped forward and embraced me silently. It started to rain. I heard the door shut and the engine start. I saw the women of my family huddled together in the doorway of Möbelhaus Weyrich. I saw Opa standing silently, several yards away. I felt a stab of pity. I had never seen him look so lonely.

*

'Don't worry,' said the man at the consulate. 'All your relations will be there to meet you at the airport. They've been looking forward to seeing you for years.' I wasn't convinced. If Mother was so keen to see me, why hadn't she written for so long? Who were all these relations? Aunty Hilda was dead, and I couldn't think of any other relatives apart from Robin. Did they mean *he* would be there to welcome me? When was I going? Not for some weeks, as it turned out. The railway system was still disrupted, and I would have to go by aeroplane. There was tremendous competition for places, and I would have to wait until there was a flight with room to take me. Meanwhile, the consulate had organised a place in a displaced persons' camp in Frankfurt. The driver who had collected me had been instructed to take me there. I would be perfectly comfortable, and in any case I wouldn't be there long.

Neither of these assertions turned out to be true. The camp was housed in several large blocks of flats that the British had requisitioned for the purpose. My driver stopped outside one of them and helped me carry my bag up several flights of stairs to an attic room that had been kitted out as a dormitory.

About thirty people were lying about aimlessly on bunks. A cloud of cheap tobacco smoke hung in the air. A group of unshaven men were playing cards on an upturned box in one corner. They were gabbling to each other in a language that I could neither recognise nor understand. I chose an unoccupied bottom berth in the opposite corner. By the time I had put my bags beside the pile of sheets and blankets on it, the driver had gone. I made up the bed, kicked off my shoes, and climbed into it. I turned my face to the wall and pretended to be asleep.

I spent much of the next fortnight lying in that bed with my back to unwashed strangers as they argued, cried, snored, sang drunkenly, or furtively made love. Anywhere had to be better than this – even England. After a couple of weeks, I was rescued by an English couple who had been billeted in a small room next to the dormitory. Seeing how depressed I was, they took pity on me and invited me to share their room, in which there was just enough space for me to put my mattress on the floor. They were German speakers, and they listened appreciatively when I told them about my life and family in Miltenberg. Then they told me about things that had been happening in Germany of which I knew nothing. They spoke of gas chambers built to eliminate millions of men, women and children. They told me of unspeakable tortures visited upon the innocent, of the secret murders of the mentally handicapped, of the casual executions of countless political opponents at home and in all the countries occupied by Hitler's Reich.

I didn't believe them.

10

An Outcast

1941–45

I've no patience with them. They were better off as they were in the old days, treated hard. When your back's sore with sleeping on boards you haven't time to think of your troubles.

Catherine Dee, *No Complaints in Hell*

I know what Mother's imprisonment was like because she wrote about it – not in *Daemons and Magnets*, in which all she says of the years 1941 to 1945 is that they amounted to 'a dreary time of mundane occupations, with nothing to enliven it but the hope of peace', but in her first published novel, *No Complaints in Hell*. She omitted the experience from her autobiography entirely. Her daemons had driven her to embrace a cause that had earned her humiliation; her magnets had drawn her to personal defeat. Her pride did not allow her to admit it. The blurb on the dust jacket of *No Complaints in Hell* describes it as a novel pervaded by an air of 'absolute reality'. What most readers would not know is that the book is so convincing because so much of it is true. Her description of a first night as a remand prisoner is written from experience:

[She] followed the motley collection up several flights of stone steps to the reception cubicles; and in one of these structures, like a horse-box, with a wooden plank running along one side of it, she prepared to spend the next two or three hours awaiting medical inspection. Another mug of tea, with bread and margarine, were thrust into her hands before she was locked in.

Opposite her, hanging on the door, was a card giving the prison diet in detail and, because she had nothing else to do, she began reading it carefully. Stewed meat, or ham or bacon, or salt fish, suet pudding, porridge, regulation rations of margarine, cheese, bread, sugar, tea, cocoa ... But it was getting dark, and the little there was to see was quickly becoming invisible. Down one side of the dirty yellow wall above the cubicle, a trickle of water meandered slowly away from the far-away, opaque skylight; the damp air of the place was penetrating through her clothes, making her tremble slightly with cold and nervous exhaustion.

The door sprang suddenly open and the doctor, a tall, over-dressed woman, with a stethoscope curiously mingling with a large fox fur slung over her shoulders, bade [her] come forward . . . The doctor placed the stethoscope against [her] throat, disregarding her efforts to make her neck more accessible, and after briefly listening, inquired if she was subject to fits, varicose veins or any discharges. Then [she] was swiftly locked in again.

It was quite dark when the door was next opened; [she] now sat huddled in a corner, her arms clasped about herself to control her violent trembling.

'Come along,' said the nurse, 'look sharp!', in the same fault-finding voice which the policewoman had used, as if nothing but the tardiness of prisoners made the long arm of the Law so slow in its manipulations. She was taken to a small room to have her head examined under a brilliant light, and then she was weighed, the nurse carefully whispering her weight to an officer sitting at a table with a pen and book.

'Now have your bath, and be quick about it. You're almost the last,' said the nurse, as if that was her fault, too.

'I wouldn't, if I was you,' whispered the prisoner acting as bath attendant. 'The water's gone stone cold. I've 'ad to get one ready for you – but just go in for a bit, and 'ave a wash.' She handed her a large, coarse cotton nightgown and a towel . . .

She passed into yet another small room, to surrender her handbag, and all her jewellery except her wedding-ring; and, at last, she entered upon the final stage of her day's journeyings. The big, high-vaulted Reception Hall, empty but for herself and the half-dozen other 'remands' and their escort, echoed to the sound of their clattering footsteps. It had the unspeakable dreariness of some vast outer chamber of Hell: a dank, dripping Inferno, festooned with sluggish water: instilled with the horror of nothingness – of not being, not seeing, not doing, and yet knowing that here was the torment of complete negation.

At the door of the Hall each woman was given a Bible to take with her to her cell. Her cell, indeed, was a haven of comfort for [her], after the basic necessities of her recent accommodation. And although the previous occupant had left cigarette ends, crumbs, fragments of a letter and a strong smell of stale tobacco smoke behind her, the sight of a wash-stand, table and chair, and a bed with sheets and blankets, was almost like a glimpse of home. Almost, but not quite; for as she lay in bed resting her throbbing feet at last, the brief illusion of comfort made her so far forget her present miseries that she stretched out a hand to put out the light, as she habitually did each night: her hand groped aimlessly for a moment above her head before she realised her mistake . . . A minute later the spy-hole clicked open, she was swiftly inspected, and her light was switched off from without. She was plunged into darkness: darkness so complete that there was nothing to do but sink heavily into it, and sleep.*

Mother served her sentence in HMP Aylesbury, where her relief at escaping a death sentence quickly turned to depression. For her, the punishment wasn't so much the loss of freedom but the boredom, which she found unbearable. She felt that there was nothing more purposeful to be done than kill time. Her fellow prisoners were employed in sewing mailbags and dresses, and – if they were lucky – in gardening. Mother was no good at any of these things, and she took no pleasure in them. She also found the prison uniform dispiriting. It wasn't so much that the shapeless, blue-grey cotton frocks and the blue serge capes worn against the weather were ugly, as that they suppressed individuality. Mother hated being forced to conform.

Prison life was dull, but it was not without emotional intensity. Mother noticed that many of the prisoners developed

*Catherine Dee, *No Complaints in Hell*, Peter Davies, 1949, pp. 34–6.

schoolgirl crushes on each other, or on those in charge of them. One of the plot lines in *No Complaints in Hell* concerns the arrival of a new governor, Helena, 'a dramatic, dazzling revelation of what Woman in Authority could be', whose glamour inspires numerous prisoners to compete for her attention.

> The virus of adoration spread rapidly. In a week's time every lavatory wall, and almost every cell in the Borstal wings, was inscribed with declarations of love for the Governor. Hearing about them, Helena ordered a general cleansing of all written matter from walls and doors; but the inscriptions were soon back again, to stay, and receive their usual concomitants of entwined hearts and crude verses.

Reading *No Complaints in Hell* now, I can see how Mother's time in prison marked a turning point. It seems to have fanned the spark of compassion that had lain hidden under her egotism. Forced to live in the company of criminal outcasts and misfits, she learned to see many of them as flawed fellow humans worthy of pity; no out-and-out Nazi could see lawbreakers in such a light. One of the main characters is Christine Parr, who has been convicted of passing secret information to the enemy. She is clearly and closely modelled upon Mother, though one essential detail has been changed. Her motivation is not fascism, but pacifism.* The other three prisoners at the centre of the story are painted

---

*Ironically, she is the least convincing figure in the book: the *Times Literary Supplement* reviewer describes her character as 'incredibly naïve'.

sympathetically, too. The shoplifter has stolen to support her pregnant daughter and ailing grandchild. The murderess has been brutalised by a cruel and neglectful mother. The back-street abortionist has taken up her profession after spending years nursing a sick husband, who died leaving her with no means of support.

No Complaints in Hell also contains some of the less attractive characters Mother met in prison, including the 'Number One Prisoner, feared, hated, admired, splendid in her isolation . . . a woman who had served a three-years' sentence for slashing her fellow-lodger's face with a razor, [and] held complete sway over officials and prisoners alike through the sheer might of her temper and vicious tongue'. Another woman 'was serving a ten years' sentence for shoot-ing her lover and throwing vitriol at her rival's face; and it was her proud boast that after doing so she had returned home and cooked her husband's supper'.

But Mother's real interest lay in her companions' frailties and kindnesses. One of the most affecting chapters describes what it was like to be behind bars at Christmas, when prisoners exchanged home-made presents – embroidered handkerchiefs and pincushions, and jars of chocolate spread made from cocoa and clarified margarine. The governor gave all the prisoners a Christmas present, too: two large buns and a cigarette for those who smoked, and three large buns for those that didn't.

> And on this hallowed day only, the power of choice was left to the women as to what they would do with their time, and where

they would go, within the limits of the prison walls. Even exercise was not compulsory, and the majority elected to forgo it. Reading, smoking, eating and talking in each other's cells – chiefly smoking and talking – were the most favoured pursuits. On no other day was it possible to smoke in this civilised fashion, slipping easefully, without thought for the morrow, from one cigarette to another in a burst of glorious fecklessness . . .

Several of the younger women went to the recreation room, where a large fire was burning, and danced to gramophone records which someone had had sent in for Christmas. They glided round the big, shabby room, whose bleakness was accentuated rather than relieved by its gaudy streamers, wearing a rapt look on their faces. Drabness and monotony and dreary reality were forgotten in this brief, illusory substitute for romantic enjoyment, afforded by another woman's arms and the sounds from a battered gramophone. When the music stopped there was a frenzied clapping for more from the half-tranced pairs bemused by the twin drugs of rhythmic movement and popular song.

There were also more dramatic manifestations of unhappiness. Mother describes a riot that is quelled with high-pressure water hoses, in which hysterical individuals are subdued by being thrashed across the face with wet towels.

Two officers [were] trying to pinion the arms of a kicking, sobbing girl with face and hands a ghastly mess of cuts and wounds self-inflicted during her 'smash-up'. Bits of china and glass were strewn about the floor and a sheet torn in shreds lay on the bed. Portraits of male film-stars, cut from magazines, hung awry but intact upon the walls – the only destructible objects in the room which had been left whole . . . The tumult was wearing itself out, like a storm dying, with desultory sobbing, and odd snatches of abuse as its last lingering echoes.

In the summer of 1945 Mother was released on licence. The terms of it are echoed in *No Complaints in Hell*, in the licence granted to Christine Parr:

> The holder . . . shall abstain from any violation of the law . . . shall not habitually associate with notoriously bad characters, such as reputed thieves and prostitutes . . . shall not lead an idle and dissolute life, without visible means of obtaining an honest livelihood . . .
>
> If she is found in or upon any dwelling-house or any building, yard, or premises . . . shop, warehouse, countinghouse . . . any garden, orchard, pleasure-ground, or nursery-ground, or in any building or erection in any garden, orchard, etc., without being able to account to the satisfaction of the court before whom she is brought . . .
>
> She shall personally notify the place of her residence to the chief officer of police of the district in which her residence is situated . . . and shall whenever she changes such residence within the same police district, personally notify such change to the chief officer . . .
>
> If she fails to comply with any of the preceding requisitions she shall either forfeit her Licence or be sentenced to imprisonment . . .

Mother's conditions were equally strict. But she was free.

Picking Up the Pieces

1945–48

SON SAFE AND WELL BEING REPATRIATED
TO CROYDON BY AIR WITHIN NEXT FEW
DAYS SIGNED FOREIGN OFFICE
Telegram received by Norah Briscoe on
2 November 1945

The Dakota landed at Croydon aerodrome with a bump. The journey had been long, noisy and uncomfortable. I had been strapped to a slatted wooden seat, flanked by two beery soldiers who had spent much of the flight shouting to each other over the roar of the engines – in English, a language I could no longer understand. We all tumbled out of the plane and down a stepladder onto the tarmac, and I followed the other passengers to the arrivals hall. One moment it was full of uniforms and smiling faces; the next it was empty, apart from me.

All I could do was wait. Night fell, and a fog rolled in. There would be no more arrivals in that weather, and the main lights in the arrivals hall were turned off. A policeman appeared and said something to me that I didn't understand, then disappeared. I took my bag out onto the front steps and looked up and down the road. Nobody. It was cold and damp and I felt utterly abandoned. At home, Opa would be feeding the *Kachelofen* and Oma and Hildegard would be setting the table for supper. I couldn't bring myself to imagine the scene. I was fifteen years old – nearly a man – but I wept. I had recovered myself by the time the policeman appeared again. He said something that sounded reassuring, and this time, he stayed.

After a while, I saw a pair of headlights cutting their way feebly through the fog that had settled like a slab over the airport. They grew brighter and a taxi drew up and stopped. Two women got out and the policeman ushered me towards them. One of them must be Mother, but which? I stepped forward and kissed the prettier one. It was the wrong choice. Mother had brought Molly with her. The policeman looked embarrassed; this clearly wasn't the joyful reunion he had expected. As I turned to pick up my suitcase, he slipped away.

Mother dismissed the cab and the three of us hurried to the bus stop. Mother wanted to chat, but I was tired, and her German wasn't very good. After a while, she gave up, and she and Molly conversed in English while I stared out of the grimy bus window at the grimier world outside. Lamp-posts and traffic lights loomed out of the mist. The pavements were empty and there was no other traffic about. Eventually, Molly got off and melted into gloomy suburbia, and Mother explained that we were very nearly 'home'. To me, the word meant a family house in a beautiful town in Bavaria. To Mother, it meant a tiny bedsit on the top floor of 72 Harrington Road, South Norwood. When she opened her front door, I asked where my room was. She explained that she only had one room, and I would have to sleep on the floor. I put down my bag, and she switched on a two-bar electric fire. She asked if I was hungry, and when I said yes, she turned the fire on its side and balanced a piece of bread on it to make toast. She didn't have a kitchen, she explained, and the house only had one bathroom. We had to share it with the occupants of the other five 'flats'. 'But why do you live like this?' I asked. 'England won the war, didn't she?' If Mother answered, I don't remember what she said.

My memories of London in 1945 are entirely monochrome. The only images I can summon up are black-and-white. Even in defeat, Miltenberg had a beauty that lifted the spirits. When the sun rose, it still sent purple and gold shimmers over the forests above, and the river valley would still fill with curds of curling mist. But November in South Norwood was colourless. The very buildings seemed to be hanging their heads in depression. Tired, bomb-broken Victorian terraces stretched in all directions. The horizon was marked by rows of sagging roofs and tilting chimney pots, from which smudges of smoke stained a sullen sky. Boarded-up windows overlooked flowerless front gardens, and gateless gateposts* opened onto featureless streets.

*Cast iron had been collected for the war effort; gates and railings had been ripped up all over London.

Mother appeared quite unmoved by all this dreariness when she led me down South Norwood High Street the following morning. She was in high spirits, for she was going to introduce me to someone she very much wanted me to meet. We stopped at a crumbling Victorian house where we knocked at a door that was answered by Molly. Standing behind her was a slightly built man with a narrow face and staring eyes. He introduced himself as Jock Houston. He seemed to think that I should recognise the name, but I didn't. He invited us in and led us down the hall to their bedsit. It was almost as small as Mother's, but it felt less claustrophobic, for it opened onto a small back yard. Molly produced some tea. I drank it with no pleasure; I was used to coffee, even if I had forgotten what real coffee tasted like. Then we all sat down, and Mother said that Jock and Molly were looking forward to hearing about my wartime experiences – but nearly all the talking that followed was done by Jock. He spoke in German; his accent was so thick that I couldn't understand half of what he was saying, but I could tell from his tone that he was dispensing wisdom, correction and advice. I had never met anyone so full of himself – except, perhaps, Herr Göpfert. Mother and Molly were obviously in awe of him. Afterwards, Mother asked me what I thought. I gave the answer that I could see was expected: that Jock was clearly a remarkable chap.

I felt no affection for the Mother that had reclaimed me, but I could see that she was genuinely proud of me. I was grateful for that. A couple of days after she had shown me off to Jock, she took me on a series of bus rides across London to present me to Dr Leigh Vaughan-Henry, assuring me that I would like him, and that he spoke perfect German. She was precisely 50 per cent correct. His German was exquisite, but his manner was so precious as to be repugnant. I can remember the exact words he used on first seeing me: '*Ah! Ein Junge aus der Heimat!*' he sighed – 'Ah! A young man from the Homeland!' I felt patronised and uncomfortable. He was dressed in a formal suit, tie and watch chain, and I could see that he was looking at my tweed jacket and skiing breeches with suppressed amusement. He talked of the beauties of Germany in general and Bavaria in particular, which made me feel homesick for the country and the people I considered my own. But I didn't tell him that. I didn't want to share my private thoughts with a stranger who made my flesh creep. He had cold eyes, like a snake's.

It was obvious that there wasn't enough room for me at Harrington Road, but finding alternative accommodation in war-damaged London was difficult. Mother got round the problem with the help of a colleague at the *Croydon Advertiser* who worked in the advertising department, who passed on an advertisement for a flat in nearby Limes Road before it was printed. It wasn't a place we would have rented if we had had a choice. The landlady was so obsessed with order and cleanliness that when she opened the front door, the smell of furniture polish and household bleach hit me in the nostrils like a fist. Her name was Mrs Channon. She wore a full set of dentures that displayed few of the qualities of real teeth. When her jaw dropped in annoyance – which was often – the top set would fall to meet the bottom, even though her mouth remained wide open. She was coldly unwelcoming to both of us, making it clear that she did not wish to see or hear us when we were in the house. When Mother was out at work, I stayed in during the day, because I couldn't venture out of the front door for fear of getting lost: I didn't speak enough English to ask directions. I sat on the bed, hardly daring to move in case I made a floorboard creak, which would prompt Mrs Channon to bang on the ceiling with a broom handle. I was hungry, lonely, frustrated and homesick for everything and everyone in and around Miltenberg. I made no effort to conceal any of these feelings from Mother. I couldn't understand why she had dragged me back to this rootless, hand-to-mouth existence. I was in the way – just as I had been when I had last lived with her.

One day, Mother told me something that cheered me up. A colleague had given her the address of a group of German expatriates who met in a church hall in Croydon. She drew me a detailed map showing how to find it, noting down the number of the bus I had to catch to get me there, and the number of stops I should count before I had to get off. She gave me the exact change for the fare there and back so that I didn't have to engage the conductor in conversation. When I found the place, I walked twice round the block before summoning up the courage to enter. People were sitting around the hall in groups, drinking coffee and chatting. I didn't know what to do, but a kindly-looking middle-aged woman saw me standing there and beckoned me over to join her and her friends at their table. They asked me where I was from, and I was soon rattling off details of the shop, Hildegard and Seppl, Opa and Oma, and Maria and Willi. A thin old man with wire-rimmed spectacles noticed the scars on my hand and asked how I had got them; I told him and he nodded sympathetically. I pointed out that my wounds had won me a medal from the Hitler Youth – at which point the people at my table fell silent, and the atmosphere suddenly changed. The old man asked me whether I realised that everybody else in the hall was Jewish. Drowning in embarrassment, I got up without answering and left.

Life in Limes Road was impossible. Mother and I conducted conversations in whispers. When Mother had to type anything at home, she did so under the eiderdown to deaden the sound of the keys. Mrs Channon, however, allowed herself total licence in the matter of noise. She was an enthusiastic but ungifted pianist who would accompany her even less accomplished singing voice at full volume whenever the mood took her – which was often. She had a snappy, sharp-eyed peke, which yelped and scratched at the door every time Mother or I entered or left the house. We couldn't go on like this for much longer. One morning, Mrs Channon ascended the stairs to tell Mother off for scuffing the newly painted hall skirting board with her shoe, and before she could finish her list of other grievances and complaints, Mother fixed her with a look of contempt and calmly gave her a week's notice. 'But where will we go?' I asked Mother, after she had shut the door in the face of our soon-to-be-ex-landlady. 'The Lord will look after us,' she said. And He did – after a fashion.

The newly opened International Club in East Croydon wasn't as grand as it sounded. Membership was far from exclusive. It was little more than a dosshouse for foreigners displaced by war. About three hundred of us were accommodated in several large Victorian houses that had been crudely divided into bedsits. We arrived on the day that the builders finished converting the last of them, so we had the pick of the empty rooms. We were invited to choose our furniture from the store in the basement and drag it up the stairs ourselves. No carpets or curtains were provided; we covered our windows with blankets. We needed to: it was winter, and the only heating came from whatever we could find to burn in our small cast-iron grate.

Bathroom facilities were shared – with residents who seemed not to have encountered lavatories or bathtubs before. The plumbing and the electricity supply failed frequently. Meals were eaten in common in a huge refectory. Our landlord was an Irishman, and he had recruited Irish waitresses to serve us at our trestle tables and benches. The poor girls seemed to feel just as far from home as I did, and they worked hard for their pocket money and keep. Mealtimes were pure theatre. There were as many ideas of table manners as there were nationalities. People ate with their fingers, drank from water jugs, and snatched at the huge piles of bread and margarine that provided the bulk of every breakfast, lunch or supper. Words had to be shouted to be heard against the background hubbub, and conversation was conducted in accents so strange that I couldn't recognise any of the few English words that I knew. But I soon realised that everybody was in the same boat. Many of the other residents spoke even less English than I did, and I found myself giving as well as receiving advice and help.

I wanted to become an architect. I had wanted to be one ever since I had looked over Willi Schwinn's shoulder as he sat working on the drawings of the gun emplacement he designed for the Eiffel Tower. Mother took me to the offices of several architects in and around Croydon, but it soon became clear that nobody wanted to take on a novice who couldn't speak the language, and in any case, trainees were required to pay a fee, which Mother couldn't afford. So Mother enrolled me on a history of architecture course at the Croydon School of Arts and Crafts. I loved it. Nobody seemed to mind my clumsy English, and I began to make friends. But after a couple of months, Mother told me she couldn't afford the fees any longer; I would have to leave and get a job. I found one as an assistant groundsman at the South Norwood Sports Club. It didn't bring me much opportunity to practise conversation, but it did earn me enough money to pay for evening classes in English. I studied hard.

Mother was regaining her self-confidence. She hated her job at the *Croydon Advertiser*, reporting on weddings and church fêtes and dog shows. She had been lucky to get any job at all: the first question at any job interview in 1945 was always 'What did you do during the war?' She had only been taken on because the editor, who had employed her in the past, had taken pity on her. But Mother was determined to do something that was worthy of her talent, and she certainly felt she deserved to live somewhere more civilised than the International Club, where she slept on a mattress supported on three tea chests cut down to form a bed. Jock and Molly had moved to Essex, where they had bought a row of dilapidated cottages to renovate. In the spring of 1947 Mother and I visited them there, and she decided there and then that we, too, should move to the country. Molly produced an advertisement she had spotted in a magazine: 'Workers wanted for community farm'. Mother answered it.

When the reply came, Mother told me excitedly that the advertiser was John Middleton Murry, the literary critic and editor of the pacifist journal *Peace News*. The name meant nothing to me, but Mother was delighted at the prospect of working for someone so famous, and believed that she was in with a chance, for Murry had been as vehemently opposed to the war as she had been, though he had shown his opposition more tactfully.* The farming 'community' he had established was mostly made up of conscientious objectors.

When Mother returned from the interview, she was exultant. She had been invited to become one of Murry's secretaries. He wanted help with his literary magazine, *The Adelphi*, and Mother was only too happy to provide it. There was work for me, too, as a farm labourer. I was to be paid ten shillings a week – though seven shillings and sixpence was to be deducted for my keep. It didn't sound like a good deal to

*Murry wrote in *Peace News* in August 1940: 'Personally I don't believe that a Hitlerian Europe would be quite so terrible as most people believe it would be.' In October 1942, he published a piece by the Marquess of Tavistock that referred to 'the very serious provocation which many Jews have given by their avarice and arrogance when exploiting Germany's financial difficulties, by their associations with commercialised vice, and by their monopolisation of certain professions'.

me, but I allowed myself to look forward to it. Murry's farm, Mother told me, was in Suffolk, where the countryside was beautiful. It had to be better than living in South Croydon, where the drabness was a constant drain on my spirits.

Our employment was to start as soon as was convenient, and a week later, we gathered together our few possessions and made the train journey from Liverpool Street to Diss. The landscape in between was flat and undramatic, but it was open, free and unscarred by war. Murry met us at the station. Slightly built, balding and bespectacled, he seemed friendly and relaxed, introducing himself as 'John'. He chatted easily with Mother as he drove us to Lodge Farm, Thelnetham. I don't know what they were saying, but there was much laughter. It was a long time since I had heard anybody laughing. I dared to hope that things might turn out well in Suffolk – not just for me, but for Mother, too.

The farmhouse was a handsome, thatched building flanked by laburnum and lilac trees in full bloom. We were introduced to Phyllis, the housekeeper – a good-natured, garrulous woman in her forties – and invited to join the rest of the community for tea on the lawn. We met Dougall, the farm foreman, a tall, red-haired, strong and bearded Scotsman who worked day and night like Boxer, the horse in *Animal Farm*. He and his family lived in a little cottage nearby. We met Paul, the cowman, who lived in the village. The rest of the workers all lived in the main farmhouse. There was Gladys, the ex-landgirl, Harold, the horseman, Johnny, the tractor driver and mechanic, and Trevor, the poultryman. Last to be introduced was a strongly built, shy-looking man of about thirty who was sitting on a folding chair in the shade of the hedge. When he got up to greet us and told us that his name was Franz, I realised that he was German and as far away from home as I was. We became friends instantly. He told me that he was a PoW who was allowed out of the camp at nearby Redgrave Hall at weekends to act as the farm's blacksmith.

The next day was a Sunday, and things were looking good. I had slept well in a comfortable bed. The sun was shining and the weather was set fair. When Mother and I went down to the kitchen, Phyllis was serving breakfast: porridge, scrambled eggs, toast and marmalade and tea. Harold and Johnny were already at table, and they cheerfully invited us to join them. Once again, it seemed, I was part of an extended family – more like the real one at Miltenberg than the chaotic collection of refugees at the Croydon International Club.

Gladys came in after finishing the milking and asked us whether we would be going to church: not the village one, she explained, but 'John's' – the John in question being John Middleton Murry. It was the custom in his community for everyone to be known by his or her first name. Gladys explained that on Sundays John presided at divine service in a first-floor room in the farmhouse. Everybody else would be there, and we would be very welcome to join them. Mother accepted the invitation on our behalf.

The room seemed suitably churchlike. It had Gothic leaded windows at one end. But the altar that stood in front of the windows was odd. It looked like a workbench, and though there was a cross on it, there was also a large, old-fashioned jack-plane. When John entered through a side door, he was

vested in sandals and a woodworker's apron. The symbolism
was obvious, even to me. We were in the presence of Jesus, the
carpenter of Nazareth. I couldn't understand the words of the
service. Dougall and Harold took turns to read from a bible on
the lectern, then John preached a sermon at some length. I
had no idea of what he was saying, but Mother did. She
recorded her interpretation of his preachings in *Daemons and
Magnets*:

> As far as I could gather from the eloquent, exalted outpouring,
> the chilling message was that there was no benevolent God to
> help us, but only Christ, the perfect man: a hearty schoolboy,
> with a love not only for his fellow men, but for a square deal and
> a true pal, laughter (without cruelty, of course) and loyalty.
> Cheats he abhorred, but with a sense of shame for them, and for
> the chap who let him down; for he had a passion for justice, this
> hero of John's, as he had for love. And yet this lovely chap, this
> spirit of liberated Man, had been let down by the father he, like
> us, had been led to believe was God. 'My God!' had he not cried
> out on the cross? 'Why hast thou forsaken me?' The God in
> whom he had believed and trusted did not exist, after all. He had
> sacrificed his life to a gigantic hoax, a myth.
>
> And so we had come to be members of a free society, away
> from the corrupt world, misled by myth and materialism: to be
> regenerated, made whole. We had come to work until it hurt for
> our ideals (and John's) without thought of profit for our
> labours – although rewards would come, in due course, our
> cups brimming over with the fruits of the earth as Christ had
> promised, if only we would believe in Love.

I am not sure I would have made much sense of John's teachings even if my English had been perfect. But I soon realised that our community was cut off from the rest of the world, and I quickly found out what it meant to work until it hurt. And I could see for myself that our cups were not brimming over with the fruits of the earth. The housekeeper fed us on various combinations of vegetables served with Yorkshire pudding. There was gravy, but very little meat in our diet. I had eaten better on *Eintopf* Sundays in Miltenberg.

Life at Lodge Farm was hard, but I was too busy to be unhappy – though I didn't take naturally to farming. One day, I was sent out with Maggie the Suffolk Punch mare, hitched up to a hay rake. Dougall came out with me and showed me how to row up hay for baling, and then left me to it. I knew how to work the reins, but lacked the confidence to let the horse know who was in charge. She set her own pace, far too fast for me to be able to work the pedals to gather the hay into tidy lines. After the first turn, I had left not a row of hay, but several huge balls of it; after the second, I had produced a series of ragged wisps. Before I knew it, we had finished, and the horse decided that she had earned the right to eat her fill from the neighbouring field of fodder beet. No amount of shouting or tugging would stop her, and as she cantered through the gateway, a wheel hub caught on the post. She reared, threw me and the rake into the ditch, then galloped off with the shafts still hanging on her harness.

We were an odd bunch at the farm. Trevor was a habitual gambler who knew more about racehorses than the poultry he was paid to look after. Johnny the tractor man was a talented pianist who would often play late into the night. Gladys doted on him, and would sit by him for hours before the two of them would tiptoe upstairs to bed. One hot day, I saw Gladys driving the farm's ancient Bedford lorry while stripped to the waist, completely unselfconscious. Her breasts trembled with the shaking of the engine. I wondered if Margaret's breasts looked like that.

Margaret was the girl from the village who helped out in the house and the kitchen. She had dark hair and eyes as bright as cherries. I used to find excuses to linger wherever she was working. I thought my admiration for her was secret, but I now wonder if the others noticed me hanging around her like a puppy. I couldn't believe my luck when she asked me whether I wouldn't be more comfortable lodging with her family for five shillings a week. When I told Mother, she told me that I should accept the offer gratefully. I am sure that she, at least, had no idea of my romantic interest. Margaret's parents were poor, but generous. They fed me well. Her father, 'Digger' Thurlow, was the parish sexton. Soon after I moved in, he was taken ill and I helped him out by digging several graves on his behalf. It was harder work than I imagined. The soil was heavy clay with chalk and flints. I started the first one at lunchtime, and was still digging in the midsummer dark. But I didn't mind. I was sacrificing myself for the father of the lovely Margaret. I was sure that sooner or later, she would notice my love for her and respond to it. But she never did. The only person I ever got close to at Lodge Farm was Franz. He was the only real farmer among us, and he had a natural feel for the land. He taught me how to plough a straight furrow, controlling the horses with simple, firm commands.

Franz had an English girlfriend with whom he was conducting a rather more successful relationship than I was with Margaret. One day, he asked me if I could do him a favour on my half-day off. Could I please get him a *Verhütungsmittel* from the chemist? I knew what he wanted, but I hadn't yet learned the English word 'contraceptive', and I was mortified at the thought of buying such a thing myself. But he had been so kind to me, and I felt I couldn't let him down. I cycled to Diss and found a chemist shop. A middle-aged man was serving behind the counter, but as I approached him, he turned away, and his place was taken by a pretty blonde girl scarcely older than I was. I felt myself blushing, but there was no going back. I had prepared a little speech involving the words 'intercourse', 'prevent' and 'baby', but when it came to it, I was overcome with embarrassment. I heard myself say, ridiculously, 'Please can I have a balloon for a man?' and the girl looked puzzled, and called back the pharmacist. He knew what I wanted – my blushes probably conveyed my meaning more than my words did – and he produced a little packet from under the counter. When I handed it to Franz, he gave me a knowing wink.

*

Mother and I left Lodge Farm in 1947. The leaving wasn't easy. There was something cultish about the Middleton Murry community. There was an unspoken understanding that we were all under a moral obligation to stay. What moved

Mother to think the unthinkable was the sudden departure of Gladys, who told her one day that she had had enough and was going to quit. She couldn't bring herself to tell John of her decision; she was going to slip away the following morning after milking the cows. Mother was braver: she writes in *Daemons and Magnets* of how she told Murry to his face that she had found another job:

> It was strange how difficult we renegades found it to confront that mild, gentle man, and the puzzled, sadly accusing eyes, to tell him the unpalatable truth: that his free society felt remarkably like a prison to us, from which we must escape or die. One after another we deserted him that summer – except for what he proudly called his 'hard core' who remained to confirm his faith in himself as a reborn Christ.

The job Mother had found was as an assistant matron in a Land Army hostel on the border between Suffolk and Essex. It came with accommodation and keep. The responsibilities were light. She had little to do but hand out aspirins and sticking plasters, and check that the girls hadn't smuggled boyfriends into the dorms. But there was a pastoral aspect to the post, too, and Mother rose to the challenge. She found herself genuinely caring for those in her charge. She was changing; *Daemons and Magnets* shows it. The one-time admirer of the master race found herself taking pity on two Latvian refugees who the hostel's head warden had written off as 'moronic peasants', but whom Mother saw as 'industrious, amiable women exiled from their own country, all their relations killed by war'.

Their fortitude and their touching gratitude for the portable gramophone and records I lent them were pathetic. Lacking newspapers or books they could read, they usually spent their spare time in bed.

Mother could see that the women were depressed, and did what she could to encourage them and cheer them up. It worked.

In time, thank God, the 'peasants' picked up some English and spent their free days in the nearest town, and attained some dignity in the eyes of their fellow-serfs.

Mother's concern for the underdog was genuine, and is reflected in *No Complaints in Hell*, which she finished in the autumn of 1948. She sent the typescript to Peter Davies Ltd, a publishing house that had responded encouragingly to samples of work she had sent them before the war. This time, the reply came from Peter Davies* himself, who wrote offering to accept her novel, which he said indicated that she had 'the real stuff of the novelist' in her. Mother was delighted. Davies asked whether he was right in assuming that it was 'based upon personal experience', in which case there might be 'some small risks of libel'. He had the typescript read by 'an exceedingly capable (and, may I add, appreciative) lawyer' who wanted to meet Mother to talk through one or two points. The meeting took place over lunch, and in her thank-you letter, Mother described the occasion as 'very helpful and stimulating'. The lawyer's name was Rubenstein. Mother was no longer the 'Jew-

*The publisher who had as a child been one of J.M. Barrie's 'Lost Boys'.

wise' extremist for whom Leigh Vaughan-Henry had written letters of introduction in 1939.

The book got mixed reviews. Most praised its realistic description of prison life, but described the characterisation as functional and flat. Perhaps the most telling comment of all was made by the reviewer in the *Times Literary Supplement*, who described the character based upon Mother as 'unconvincing in her naïvety'. It was an interesting insight: Mother was beginning to understand other people, but she had not yet learned to understand herself.

While Mother was working and living in the hostel, I had digs in nearby Stoke-by-Nayland. My English was still far from perfect, but I was confident enough to apply for a job as a junior draughtsman with the Essex planning department. At the interview, they offered me the position, and I eagerly accepted – but when the official letter arrived a couple of days later, it was to explain that the offer had been withdrawn. They had noticed that my age meant I would shortly be called up for National Service. I was heartbroken – and I had no idea what National Service meant. When I asked Mother about it, she explained that I would have to join the army. I could hardly believe it, but she assured me that it was true. I could, though, refuse to serve if I could persuade them that I was a conscientious objector. Mother helped me fill in the appropriate forms, and we waited to see what would happen next. Meanwhile, I got myself a job as a handyman at Polstead Hall,* a country club in the next village.

*Famous for the nineteenth-century 'murder in the barn' of Maria Marten by the son of the squire.

The war had been over for three years now, but there were still German PoWs who had not been repatriated, and some of them were in a camp in Stoke-by-Nayland. By this time, the regime there was pretty relaxed; it was more of a hostel than a prison. Provided the men did the farm work they were allocated, they were pretty much left to themselves. Strictly speaking, they weren't supposed to fraternise with the locals, but many of them did, and I often fell into conversation with them.

One Saturday afternoon I met a couple of them in the lane; they told me that they were having a film show that evening and invited me to come along. They didn't know what the film was, but to me, it didn't matter. I still yearned for Germany, and I knew that when the lights were lowered and the projector started whirring, I would be able to imagine myself sitting in the Mainstrasse cinema, with the cobbled streets of Miltenberg just the other side of the door, and Möbelhaus Weyrich on the Marktplatz just along the road. But when the film flickered into life, on a bedsheet drawing-pinned to the hut wall, I caught my breath. As the music wound itself up to speed, the words that filled the makeshift screen were *Spiel im Sommerwind*. I suppose it wasn't as much of a coincidence as it first seemed: it must have been one of only a few films made in Germany since 1934 that weren't overtly political. But the title sequence caught me completely by surprise, and I watched the story unfolding in front of me with growing excitement. The plot moved to Miltenberg, and there was the river, and the castle, and the Marktplatz, and the fountain, and a girl with pigtails being chased around it by a boy in shorts with white-blond hair. I couldn't help it: I let out what I thought was going to be a cry of joy, but before it left my throat it turned into a sob. That boy was happy. That boy was carefree. That boy was me.

Epilogue

1948–99

Seen as a whole, life is quite a tidy business, mis-managed though it may be at times. The people who have cavorted on these pages, including me, have followed a pattern, circuitous but inevitable, like the meanderings of an intricately designed shell.

Norah Briscoe, *Daemons and Magnets*

It took a long time to become English again. While we were waiting to hear whether I would be excused National Service, Mother came into a small inheritance, and she used it to go halves with Molly and Jock on a project to renovate a terrace of four tumbledown cottages in Suffolk. Mother and I lived in one of them while Jock and I did up the rest. I ended up doing most of the donkey work, but Jock was always around to issue instructions and offer advice. There was nothing, it seemed, in which he did not claim to be an expert: politics, religion, painting, plastering, plumbing, carpentry; the list was endless. He also told me that he had the answer to my National Service problem. It was obvious. If my appeal was refused, I should take the ferry to Northern Ireland, and then slip over the border and lie low. The absurdity of the idea was obvious, even to me. What would happen when I wanted to come back? Jock said that if I kept out of sight for a few years, I would be forgotten about, but I didn't believe him. There was no point in arguing. Jock had spoken, and that was that.

Jock was a fool, but there was no telling him anything. He was always sounding off about the Jews. I had heard it all before in Germany. Now, in England, the only person I ever heard talk like that was Jock. He turned up one day with a book, telling me it contained proof that everything he had said was true. I still have it: *The Protocols of the Learned Elders of Zion*, translated from the Russian of Nilus by Victor E. Marsden, 'formerly Russian Correspondent of the *Morning Post*'.* I didn't read it. I haven't read it since.

The more I saw of Jock, the more I disliked him; the more I disliked him, the more I disliked myself. The last time I had heard talk like his, I had gone along with it. Hearing it again, I could see how even as a child, I should have recognised it for what it was. I began to feel guilty. When I had seen the films and the photographs of the bodies and the ovens and the camps, I had been horrified, but I hadn't thought of them as having anything to do with me. Forced to listen to Jock's ravings, I realised how wrong I had been to allow such hate-

*Published by the Britons Publishing Society; the edition Jock gave me was the 1936 reprint. Sergei Aleksandrovich Nilus (1862–1929) was an obsessive anti-Semite and conspiracy theorist.

speak to go unchallenged. Yes, I had my excuses: I was young; I was taught these things by my teachers; and when I asked what was happening to the Jews, I accepted what I was told by my family – that it was none of my business. But I should have made it my business. I began to be haunted by the memory of the part I had played in the desecration of the Miltenberg synagogue. I had known what I was doing was wrong, and I had enjoyed it.

Meanwhile, Mother's anti-Semitism simply evaporated. She listened politely enough to Jock's Jew rants, but I never heard her join in or concur, and I never heard her utter an anti-Semitic remark. At the time, I thought nothing of it, because I didn't then know of her reputation as an extremist among extremists. Today, I find myself wondering how her obsession could have been so easily forgotten. I can only guess, because she never talked about it. I suspect that it simply ceased to matter. Now that she was a published novelist, she had the recognition that she had craved. She didn't need the world to be turned on its head so that it would accept her as a person of importance. The idea that there was an international Jewish conspiracy to keep good people down had become irrelevant, because she no longer needed anyone to blame for her failure, now that she saw herself as a success.

My bid for conscientious objection was rejected, and I did two years' National Service – in Germany, where my knowledge of the language was put to good use. I was assigned to Field Security, put in civilian clothes and sent to listen in on political meetings. I wasn't any better at spying than Mother. I was identified as a foreigner at a gathering of old Party comrades in Bad Harzburg and was lucky to get away before I was lynched. The same thing happened at a Communist rally in Hamburg, when I was rescued by being bundled into a jeep by the Military Police.

On leave in 1950, I revisited Miltenberg. When Hildegard opened the door, she burst into tears of joy and cried out, '*Das Paulchen ist hier!*' But it wasn't true: I wasn't 'little Paul' any more. Möbelhaus Weyrich hadn't changed, but I had – though I still loved the family who had accepted me as one of their own and now warmly welcomed me back. What was their news? Seppl had turned up just two days after I had left Miltenberg. If he had got home just forty-eight hours earlier, my life would have taken a very different turn in 1945. He had been posted 'missing in action' in Yugoslavia because he had switched sides and spent the last months of the war fighting with Tito's partisans. Oma seemed to think this amusing, but I was shocked at what I thought of as treachery. Willi's career as an architect had flourished: he had designed the bridge built to replace the one destroyed by our own troops in 1945. Hildegard and Seppl hadn't had the child they had wanted; they feared they never would.* There was no new generation to inherit the family business. They were adamant: I should come home – my future was with Möbelhaus Weyrich. I didn't know how to tell them that nothing could be further from the truth. It was my past that was with them and the shop. I wanted to make my own way in the world, though I

---

*In due course, they did have a child: a son, Christian. Had I decided to return to Möbelhaus Weyrich, things would have been complicated.

had no idea what that way would be. I said I would have to think about their offer, but I had already made my decision.

So, when I was demobbed in 1951, I returned to England – and to Mother, whose novel had earned her enough money to buy a tumbledown cottage in Marlesford, east of Ipswich, but not enough to live on; the only other income she had was for a column on village life she wrote for the *East Anglian Daily Times*. It suited us both for me to move in and get a job that would pay the household bills while she worked on her next book.* I found work, first as a relief cowman, and then as a builder. I began to fit in – and Mother did, too.

We were welcomed into the community by the vicar, the Revd Mark Meynell, a kindly man who recognised Mother's isolation and my lack of self-confidence. He and his wife took us both under their wing, and we soon found ourselves part of village life. Mother was only too willing to play the part of the village 'writer', a role that was as much of an observer as a participant. She saw herself as a 'character', an interesting misfit – like the extraordinary Flora Sandes, who lived in the next village, and who had fought in the Serbian army in the Great War. Mother sought her out and befriended her.

I joined in village life more actively. The vicar ran an amateur dramatics group and I became a member. I also sang in his choir. We performed at the village Coronation party in 1953, an event at which everyone celebrated being British in a thoroughly English way. Long trestle tables were set out in the grounds of Marlesford Hall and covered with plates of home-

Nothing is Chance was published in 1952.

made sponges, jellies and sandwiches. There were party games and races for the children, stalls and sideshows, laughter, chatter and music, bunting and flags. There was no marching, stamping or saluting; the only uniforms on show were those of the village bobby and a handful of boy scouts. At the same time, all over the country, other communities were celebrating in similar ways, not because they had been ordered to, but because they wanted to. The nation was united in celebration, and it was celebrating in one great village fête. In Marlesford, and, I guess, at most of the other thoroughly gentle gatherings that day, the grand finale was the singing of the national anthem. I sang it with feeling.

In 1954, Mother's third novel was published. The blurb on the dust jacket of *Never Carry the Donkey* describes it as 'a plea for individualism, a plea that it is the right and duty of everyone to carve his own destiny, free from the interference of others'. It is not a plea that could have been made by a writer who still embraced Nazism. The following year, Mother decided to carve out her own destiny among the expatriate writers and artists on the Mediterranean island of Ischia, where she hoped to find inspiration for another book. The community included the composer Sir William Walton and the poet W.H. Auden.* Mother met them, but she did not become part of the island's artistic inner circle – she was later to joke that her only real claim to literary fame was that her dog had mated with Walton's on the beach.

---

*   . . . my thanks are for you,
         Ischia, to whom a fair wind has
     brought me rejoicing with dear friends

Meanwhile, I had fallen in love with a pretty girl at a dance in the Assembly Rooms in Framlingham. I introduced her to Mother in early September, just before she left for Italy. Monica was a primary-school teacher; her father was a farmer. I got myself a job repairing ancient monuments for the Ministry of Works; having a steady income meant I was able to ask Monica to marry me. The wedding was in August 1956. Mother didn't return for it.

We didn't see Mother again until 1960, when she returned to England after falling ill. She hadn't found artistic inspiration in Ischia, but she had met up with an old German boyfriend, Kuno – though the relationship had eventually faltered. She never did reconcile her self-centredness with her need to be loved. An English neurologist told her that she had been suffering from Bell's palsy, but that there was nothing to worry about. She would have to learn to live with a slight facial paralysis. Molly insisted that Mother shouldn't accept her condition as incurable, encouraging her to visit faith healers. Needless to say, no good came of it.

By this time, I had done a two-year teacher training course and found myself a post teaching woodwork at a secondary modern school in Essex. Mother had nowhere to live and no income. We now had a baby, Catherine, so there wasn't a spare room in our little cottage. Monica's father got hold of a

from soiled productive cities. How well you correct
our injured eyes, how gently you train us to see
   things and men in perspective
    underneath your uniform light . . .
W.H. Auden, 'Ischia', 1948

caravan, and we put it in the back garden and invited Mother to stay in it. We stayed there for twelve years, during which time I was put in charge of the Duke of Edinburgh's Award Scheme. When I accompanied some of my students to Buckingham Palace to receive their Gold Award, I was presented to Prince Philip. I did not tell him how similar his scheme was to the practical side of the training I had received as a member of the Hitler Youth.

Monica inherited a share in the family farm near Framlingham on her father's death in 1975, and we moved into the farmhouse. Mother came too. She stayed with us for the last thirty years of her life, living contentedly on the edge of our family and social circles, becoming known and liked as a spirited, independent-minded character who travelled the countryside on her bicycle until well into her eighties. She loved telling our children and our visitors stories of her life and adventures, but she never spoke of her crime or its punishment, and she fell silent whenever anyone mentioned the war.

Our visitors occasionally included Jock and Molly. Molly attended a spiritualist church in Ipswich and persuaded Mother to accompany her. In the late 1980s Molly found a lump on her breast and went to a faith healer, who prescribed prayer and a diet consisting entirely of grapes. The lump was cancerous and the cancer spread. Mother writes touchingly of Molly's death in *Daemons and Magnets*. Theirs was a genuine friendship, perhaps the only really deep and lasting relationship that Mother enjoyed. Jock was heartbroken. Mother saw less and less of him, eventually losing touch.

In 1989 we held a party to celebrate Mother's ninetieth birthday. She loved being the centre of attention and was as bright and entertaining as ever. Someone produced a violin and she gave a short impromptu concert. Her fingers were no longer nimble and she didn't play well, but we all applauded and she took a graceful bow. Her strength was beginning to fail, but not her spirit. In a letter to an old friend she wrote: 'I am not a good subject for increasing years and invalidism, for inside me rages an unquenchable teenager which has never been tamed, and nobody but myself realises it.'

In 1993 Mother suffered a series of minor strokes that left her needing constant nursing care, and we found a place for her in a home near Saxmundham. Monica and I visited her almost daily, but visits were difficult: she suffered frequent hallucinations, and would talk about strange things that only she could see. Once, she asked me the name of the woman sitting knitting in the corner of her room. There was nobody there. Another time, after the doctor had called, she said that the gold and silver tinsel with which he had decorated his coat made him look ridiculous. I told her that she was mistaken and that it must have been a trick of the light, but she dismissed my explanation as nonsense. Her visions grew increasingly bizarre. On one occasion, she pointed to a fellow patient, and said, 'Look! She's got flowers growing out of her head!' There was no point in arguing. Sometimes she imagined herself to be on board a ship in high seas; at other times she complained of being annoyed by non-existent 'blue ducks with red eyes'.

After a few months of this, she had another stroke that

robbed her of the power of speech. At first, she was distressed and frustrated, but after only a few days, she seemed to accept her condition and put up with it bravely. For the first time in her life, she was forced to be a listener rather than a talker – and it seemed to bring her a kind of peace. The garrulous, opinionated persona she had created for herself no longer existed. The vulnerable person that had hidden behind it was finally revealed. Her last weeks were a time of healing. I sat with her for several hours every day, talking about the adventures we had shared before and after the war that had separated us. I could see that this brought her pleasure: she didn't have enough movement in her face to manage a smile, but her eyes brightened, and when I stopped, she squeezed my hand to ask me to carry on.

I was holding her hand when she died. She just closed her eyes and relaxed her grip. A wave of sadness washed over me, but I didn't weep. We had grown close at the end, but it wasn't the closeness of a mother and child; it was more like the kind of friendship that springs from common experience. Mother had never given me affection – I don't think she ever once kissed or embraced me – but she had put me in the care of a family who offered the love that I needed and which she knew she couldn't provide. She had made mistakes, but she had paid for them; she had put me in circumstances in which I had made mistakes, from which I had learned. I can't blame her for what I did in the Miltenberg synagogue: I was old enough to know what I was doing was wicked. I didn't admit my guilt in the first confession that I made soon afterwards, but I admit it now: what I did was a sin – a small part of one of the greatest sins of all time, which could never have happened without many lesser sins like mine. May God forgive me for it.

*

Hildegard died in 1999. I visited her a couple of weeks before her death. She had spent several years in a nursing home run by nuns in Miltenberg. When I telephoned to say I was coming, they warned me not to expect too much. She was bedridden, paralysed and unable to understand or communicate. She had been like that for some months. She wouldn't recognise me.

It broke my heart to see her lying there, her body tidily arranged by another's hands, like a laid-out corpse. Her head was propped up slightly, facing the door. Her eyes were open, but dull and sightless. As I looked at her sunken face, a whole series of images flashed across my mind, like a rapid slide-show: a smiling Hildegard greeting customers in Möbelhaus Weyrich; Hildegard at prayer on the Walldürn and Engelberg pilgrimages; Hildegard hugging a frightened boy in the family cellar during an air raid, and later, lovingly dressing that boy's injured hand; Hildegard smiling joyfully when that boy, now a man, turned up at her door in British uniform in 1950. And now, Hildegard dying – hollow-faced, silent, exhausted.

'*Hildegard*,' I said – but she showed no sign of hearing. '*Hildegard – dein Paulchen ist hier.*'

And a large tear formed in the corner of her eye, rolled down her cheek and fell to stain the starched white pillowcase below.